高职高专"十一五"规划教材

Contemporary Business English An Integrated Course

当代商务英语
综合教程 2

总 主 编	何兆熊
本册主编	吴 慧
编 者	吴 慧　刘自中
	张校勤　孙友义

华东师范大学出版社

图书在版编目(CIP)数据

当代商务英语综合教程 2 练习与测试 / 吴慧主编. —上海:华东师范大学出版社,2008.1

高职高专"十一五"规划教材

ISBN 978 - 7 - 5617 - 5863 - 2

Ⅰ. 当… Ⅱ. 吴… Ⅲ. 商务—英语—高等学校:技术学校—习题 Ⅳ. H319.6

中国版本图书馆 CIP 数据核字(2008)第 016603 号

当代商务英语综合教程2练习与测试

主　　编　吴　慧
策　　划　高等教育分社外语部
项目编辑　李恒平
文字编辑　李恒平
责任校对　王秀娥
装帧设计　孙　箐　新月创意

出版发行　华东师范大学出版社
社　　址　上海市中山北路 3663 号　邮编 200062
客服电话　021 - 62865537(兼传真)
门市(邮购)电话　021 - 62869887
门市地址　上海市中山北路 3663 号华东师范大学校内先锋路口
销售业务电话　高教分社 021 - 62235021　021 - 62237614(传真)
　　　　　　　基教分社 021 - 62237610　021 - 62602316(传真)
　　　　　　　教辅分社 021 - 62221434　021 - 62860410(传真)
　　　　　　　综合分社 021 - 62238336　021 - 62237612(传真)
　　　　　　　北京分社 021 - 62235097　021 - 62237614(传真)
　　　　　　　　　　　010 - 82275258　010 - 82275049(传真)
编辑业务电话　021 - 62572474
网　　址　www.ecnupress.com.cn

印 刷 者　华东师范大学印刷厂
开　　本　787×1092　16 开
印　　张　6.5
字　　数　126 千字
版　　次　2008 年 3 月第 1 版
印　　次　2008 年 3 月第 1 次
书　　号　ISBN 978 - 7 - 5617 - 5863 - 2/H·376
定　　价　14.80 元

出 版 人　朱杰人

编者说明

《当代商务英语综合教程》第一至四册为基础阶段精读教材,供高职高专商务英语专业或应用英语专业学生使用,也可供程度相当的自学者使用。

英语语言基础在商务英语教学中的重要地位和作用是显而易见的。在经济全球化浪潮的冲击下,各种涉外工作对外语人才特别是商务英语人才的要求越来越高。这也对教学和教材编写提出了更高的要求。由于高职高专商务英语教学研究起步较晚等多方面原因,相关院校出现了教材跟不上形势的情况,甚至出现用《大学英语》代替"商务英语综合"或"精读"教学的极端个案。针对这些状况,我们编写本系列教材,希望能对解决这些问题做出我们微薄的贡献。

本教程以高等职业技术学院、独立本科院校商务英语专业学生入学水平的中等程度为起点,即在学习本教程之前,学生已掌握基本的英语语音和语法知识,能认知 1 900 个左右的英语单词(掌握其中 1 200 个),并在听、说、读、写等方面受过初步训练。在学完本教程后,力争做到:中上等水平的学生在英语语言知识和语言的实际运用能力方面,可以达到商务英语中高级、高等学校英语专业第四级结束时的水平,能够从事一般商务英语工作;中等水平的学生能够达到商务英语中级、大学英语六级水平,能够用英语从事相关的商务工作。

本教程的编写指导思想是全面打好学生英语基础,以课文为中心,由浅入深,循序渐进,进行语音、语法、词汇等基础知识的综合教学;对学生的听、说、读、写、译等基本技能进行全面的训练,培养学生准确运用所学知识进行语言交际的能力。

教材的质量关系到国家人才的培养。为了编写出高质量的教材,本教程编写者怀着强烈的质量意识,踏踏实实、一丝不苟地工作,在整体编写中遵循如下理念:

丰富而实用的选材。精读教材课文的核心地位为英语教学者所公认,因此我们在选材上付出的努力最多。本教程的所有课文力求内容丰富,题材各异,主题贴近生活与商务实际,视角触及面广,关注实用性。实用性体现在既选取语言优美的范文,又选取与商务相关的可读性强的短文。此外,选材的真实性是我们对实用性最好的注解之一。本教程充分利用了国外教材和相关读物以及互联网的丰富资源,其中相当部分数据、图表、商务文件、信函、产品说明书、广告、公告、通知及案例等均来自一些企业、公司或网络,并配有相当数量的练习或交际任务,旨在努力创造条件为学生提供真实的语言输入和输出机会,使学生真切地掌握相应的英语语言基础知识,熟悉商务实践的技能、策略以及相关的现实商务活动的真实场景,从而可以使学生真切地掌握相应的英语及商务实践的技能。

精心而系统的练习。练习设计的重要性不亚于课文。丰富多样的练习活动能体现各种技能训练的要求,可为学生提供更多提高听、说、读、写、译等各项技能的机会,极大地增强学生学习语言的兴趣。本教程特别突出对学生语言交际能力的培养,强调教学过程中的互动性,为学生提供了诸多在现实生活中灵活运用英语语言的场合、情景及任务等,以期达到学以致用的教学目的。

结构清晰、易于教学。教程形式活泼多样,与众不同,图文并茂,互动性强。每册教材的侧重点不同,但注意系统性和独立性的有机结合。本系列教程可成套使用,亦可根据使用者的实际情况选择使用;既适合高职商务英语专业的学生,也适用于对商务活动感兴趣的人士。

教材编写中我们还考虑了高职商务英语教学的特点,注意教材与高职教学多方面的需要相适应,考虑"两个兼顾"问题。一是实用与考试兼顾。本系列教程从选材内容到训练内容都从实用角度出发,选材内容与学生生活及社会生活息息相关;训练过程侧重学生听、说、读、写、译实用技能的培养。各册的语法、词汇、写作训练紧贴现行相关语言考试的要求,有助于学生在提高英语实际交际能力的同时,能顺利地通过大学四、六级英语考试、英语等级考试、英语专业四级等相关语言类考试。二是认知水平、系统性与可读性兼顾。在选材时,我们特别注重科学性与可读性的关系,既不失其科学的严谨性,又要考虑到学生学习心理方面的要求,力求将商务知识用浅显易懂的方式表现出来,使教材的内容具有可读性,教师愿意教,学生愿意学。

此外,与本综合教程配套使用的还有听说教程(1—4)和阅读教程(1—2)。商务英语实践性较强的听说训练均放在听说教材中;听说教程的主题与剑桥商务英语证书(BEC)以及全国商务英语认证考试紧密衔接,有助于学习者通过这些考试。商务英语阅读技能培养与实用文体阅读技巧训练这部分主要放在阅读(泛读)教材中:通过对一些商务上的数据、图表、案例、商务文书等应用性极强的材料进行全面的阅读训练,能增强学生的商务阅读能力,以适应日后所从事的各种商务实践活动。

本教程共分4册,即每学期一册。第一、二册在学生原有基础上,系统安排语音、语法等基础语言知识,其内容主要参考《高等学校英语专业基础阶段教学大纲》所列项目;第三、四册在巩固基本功的基础上,进一步加强语言实际运用能力的培养。每课授课时间可根据教学对象的水平和专业课程总体安排等情况,由教师酌定。每课内容构成如下:

- 精读课文(课文、注释、生词表、课文理解练习、与课文相关的口语活动)
- 课文练习(词汇练习、与课文相关的语法练习,本部分另见练习与测试 workbook)
- 语言在用(听力、语法练习、商务英语综合练习)
- 职业技能(第二至四册)
- 商务文体阅读课文

各部分的编写思路和使用中应注意的问题,分别说明如下:

1. Text A 精读课文

（1）鉴于学生入学水平不同，我们对课文的起点难度作了适当控制。为便于学生朗读与背诵，课文长度第一册每课一般为400—600词；第二册每课一般为500—800词；第三册每课一般为700—1 000词；第四册每课一般为900—1 400词。课文的题材内容，第一、二册以英语国家日常生活、商务活动、社会情况、百科知识、文学故事等题材为主；第三册以后，适当增加经济、科技、政治、文化等方面的内容。文体类型包括小说、散文、小品文、戏剧、传记等多种体裁，其中以叙事体为主。

（2）每课课文后列有该课生词表，每册后列有该册总词汇表。第一册后附有学生在学习本教程前应掌握的1 200个词汇及应认知的740个词汇，这些词汇所列出的含义一般不再视为生词。第一、二册全部生词采用英文、中文注释，均标注音标（少数符合读音规则的单音节生词，不注音标）；第三册开始逐渐减少中文释义。生词的中文释义力求先交代原意，再注出该词在本课中的准确含义。每册均保留4—6个一词多义的生词由学生自己查找工具书（使用英英词典），以培养学生自学习惯和独立工作的能力。课文中出现的常用搭配和习惯用法，一般单列成项，并加以注释。

（3）课文注释与理解。第一部分为课文注释，第二部分为课文理解检查题。课文注释内容包括作者简介、文章出处、语言难点和有关背景知识。课文理解检查题主要是多项选择题，供学生预习时参考，教师讲课时可据此对学生预习情况进行检查。

（4）口语实践练习。包括两个方面：一是就课文内容相互问答和围绕课文进行简单对话或专题讨论；二是在课文题材范围内模拟交际活动。

2. Additional Tasks 课文练习

（1）词汇练习。首先是借助构词法，大力扩充词汇。其次是通过介词搭配、习惯用语、短语动词、动词用法模式、同义词、一词多义等操练，打下扎实的语言基础。我们还特别强调掌握构成短语能力强的基本动词（phrasal verb）的使用，如take, make, do等动词的用法。

（2）与课文结合的语法练习。本部分练习与课文密切关联，紧紧抓住中国学生的弱项进行操练（如从句、不定式、分词、动名词、介词短语的句法作用；句子的连接；主谓一致等等）。语法项目参考《高等学校英语专业基础阶段英语教学大纲》规定的内容，逐步安排到第二册为止，每课安排一至两个重点。

（3）翻译练习。含汉译英与英译汉两种形式，目的是提升学生对语言的掌握和运用能力，注重活学活用，逐步增强学生的翻译技能。

（4）写作练习。写作实践第一册以组句、造句为主，掌握最常用的60多个句型；第二册以段落拓展为主，掌握围绕主题句写作和常用的衔接技巧（表达因果关系、进行比较、学会起承转合等等）；第三至四册以创造性写作和实用商务文体写作为主，熟悉各种写作技巧及方法（了解基本的修辞方法）。重视写作训练是本教程的重要特色之一。

3. Language in Use 语言在用

（1）听力部分。语音：在系统整理、巩固、加深已学语音知识的基础上，着重训练学生在语流中运用语音语调知识和朗读技巧。第一册前几课集中复习英语发音和读音规则；

后几课则集中回顾语调和朗读技巧训练。语感：第二、三、四册主要是通过朗读或背诵名篇名段，进一步提高学生在语流中运用语音知识和朗读技巧的能力。这一部分也充分体现了我们重视文化内涵和人文价值的思路，希望通过潜移默化的影响来培养和提升学生高尚的情操。

（2）语法部分。这部分的语法着重于帮助学生了解并巩固在商务语境下的语言表达，它与课文练习中的语法难点练习各有侧重。本部分采用教学语法的思路，以篇章为主，每课只出现语法练习，不出现讲解。有关讲解条目统一编为语法参考，放在书末。

（3）（商务）语言综合练习部分。本部分是在语篇层次上的综合练习，是教材中最有特色的亮点。所选的小文章短小精悍，材料新颖，体裁各异，语言地道，趣味性强；相当一部分材料具有强烈的时代气息和前瞻性，练习形式活泼多样。

4. Career Skills 职业技能

职业技能板块从第二册起开始出现，涵盖了商务场合中表达和沟通的各种基本职业技能训练。

5. Text B 商务文体阅读

本部分商务阅读选文注重难度适宜，文章主要选取国外同类教材、商务报刊及与商务报道相关的短文，以叙事性和描述性文体为主。第一册主要选择商业故事，主题以商务知识入门为主。第二至四册，以商务英语活动的核心主题为主线，涵盖商务语境的各个重要方面，涉及工作所需要的多个学科的知识，如：国际贸易、涉外会计、市场营销、证券投资、电子商务、经济、金融、企业管理、商业文化、信息技术、旅游等。

为了方便教师使用，本教程配备了较为详尽的教师用书。每单元的教师用书由两部分组成：第一部分是 Text explanations，该部分按课文内容的顺序把课文分为若干部分，每一部分包括 Analysis 和 Language work，为教师提供了进入课文教学时引导性的问题、讲解词汇时所需要的例句；第二部分是 Key to exercises，在必要之处我们对所给答案作了简单的解释。我们的意图是把教师用书变成一本十分实用、使用方便的教学参考书。

本教程第一至四册的主编分别为上海工商外国语（职业）学院的陈明娟副教授、上海金融学院的吴慧副教授、上海理工大学的吕乐副教授和上海立信会计学院的陈雪翎教授。青岛职业技术学院的李永生教授负责编写第一至二册"语言在用"部分的语法练习。美籍商务英语教学专家 John Parker 审定教程所有英文部分。参加本教程第二册编写工作的有吴慧、刘自中、张校勤、孙友义等老师。

本教程在编写过程中得到常玉田教授（对外经济贸易大学）、邹为诚教授（华东师范大学）、陈洁教授（上海对外贸易学院商务英语学院）、王大伟教授（上海海事大学）、张武保副教授（广东外语外贸大学商务英语学院）、井升华教授（商务英语专家）等多位英语界和商务英语教学界专家的支持，在此一并对他们表示衷心的感谢。

何兆熊
2007 年 5 月

目 录

Unit 1

Text A   The Bright Student and the Dull Student ················· 1

Unit 2

Text A   Roll Away the Stone ················· 7

Unit 3

Text A   Winners Never Quit ················· 14

Unit 4

Text A   The Praying Hands ················· 19

Unit 5

Text A   Jules Verne's Trip to the Moon ················· 25

Unit 6

Text A   What Is Happiness? ················· 31

Unit 7

Text A   Disc Jockey ················· 37

Unit 8

Text A   What's Your Spiritual IQ? ················· 42

Unit 9

Text A   Whitewashing Aunt Polly's Fence ················· 48

Unit 10

Text A   My Deep，Dark Secret ·· 54

Unit 11

Text A   The Cab Ride ·· 60

Unit 12

Text A   Civilization and History ·· 65

Unit 13

Text A   The Light Was On ·· 71

Unit 14

Text A   The Boy and the Bank Officer ·· 77

Unit 15

Text A   An Unforgettable Christmas ·· 84

Unit 16

Text A   My Father's Music ·· 90

Unit 1

Text A The Bright Student and the Dull Student

Vocabulary related to Text A

Additional Tasks

1. **Word Formation.**

   1) **Study how the word "beautify" is formed. Find out the meaning of the suffix "-fy" or "-ify" with the help of a dictionary.**

   beautify: beautiful+fy

   Fill out the table below, changing the given adjectives into verbs by adding the suffix "-fy" or "-ify".

   Example: simple (*a.*)+ify → simplify (*v.*)

adjectives	verbs	adjectives	verbs
pure		false	
ample		electric	
acid		horrible	
pretty		identical	
humid		just	

   2) **Study how the word "irregular" is formed. Find out the meaning of the prefix "ir-" with the help of a dictionary.**

   irregular: ir+regular

   Fill out the table below, changing the given adjectives into the opposite adjectives that begin with the prefix "ir-".

Example: ir＋regular (*a*.) → irregular (*a*.)

adjectives	adjectives	adjectives	adjectives
rational		religious	
relevant		reversible	
reverent		resistible	
responsible		resolute	
replaceable		repressible	

3) Complete the sentences based on the Chinese given in the brackets.

(1) I was overcome by an almost _____（不可抑制的）desire to break into song.

(2) He chose not to join his father's _____（毫不相关的）business.

(3) The subject is immensely complex，and hard to _____（简化）.

(4) She tried to _____（美化）her office with a few plants and pictures.

(5) They have found a new way to _____（净化）water.

(6) _____（无可替代的）woodland is being destroyed.

(7) The book was full of _____（不相关的）information.

(8) Such measures are easily _____（证明……有必要）and meet with approval.

(9) You have behaved like an _____（不负责任的）idiot.

(10) Many frogs _____（使……放大）the sound of their voices using special sacs（囊）in their throats.

2. Complete the sentences with the following expressions. Use the proper forms.

be curious about	get in touch with	go on	be inclined to	try out
for the time being	on the basis of	take risks		

(1) You should take your temperature and _____ you doctor.

(2) Decisions were often made _____ incorrect information.

(3) Don't forget to _____ the equipment before setting up the experiment.

(4) Don't _____, just ring the police.

(5) No one seemed _____ help.

(6) We've decided to do without a car _____ .

(7) Babies are _____ everything around them.

(8) We have never heard so much about what _____ in the company.

3. Complete the sentences with the following verbal phrases in their proper forms.

bring about	bring up	bring down	bring back	bring forth
bring out	bring forward	bring in	bring off	bring round

(1) He hasn't yet managed to _____ the others _____ to his way of thinking.

(2) The current crisis threatens to _____ the government.

(3) I was _____ by my grandmother.

(4) If he _____ the deal he'll be a wealthy man.

(5) A crisis can _____ the best in someone.

(6) The reforms are part of a series of anti-terrorist measures _____ by the government.

(7) If you _____ a few references to other authors it will make your essay more impressive.

(8) They're always campaigning to _____ the death penalty.

(9) Jealousy in a relationship is often _____ by a lack of trust.

(10) The guilty verdict has _____ sharp criticism from women's groups.

4. Examine the meanings and uses of "bright" and "dull" in the sentences below. List other possible ways of using these words, and then make sentences after the models.

Years of watching and comparing the *bright* student and the not *bright*, or less *bright*, have shown that they are very different kinds of people. (Para. 1)

The *dull* student is far less curious, far less interested in what goes on and what is real, more inclined to live in worlds of fantasy. (Para. 1)

(1) You're very **bright** and cheerful this morning.

(2) She's an excellent student with a **bright** future.

(3) When she looked up her eyes were **bright** with tears.

(4) In 1983 I moved to London, attracted by the **bright** lights of the city.

(5) Leslie always wears **bright** colours.

(6) She wrote **dull**, respectable articles for the local newspaper.

(7) He's pleasant enough, but deadly **dull**.

(8) I heard a **dull** thud from the kitchen and realized she must have fainted.

(9) The **dull** rumble of traffic woke her.

(10) She felt a **dull** ache at the back of her head.

Other possible uses of "bright" and "dull".

bright:

dull:

5. Translate the following into English，using the words given in the brackets.

(1) 他母亲还没来得及拥抱他，他便上火车了。（embrace）

(2) 请在检票处出示你的车票。（barrier）

(3) 最佳的做法就是遵守这个耳熟能详的行事准则：入乡随俗。（maxim）

(4) 我们要鞭策自己努力学习。（urge）

(5) 我不能容忍你的粗鲁。（tolerate）

(6) 他不久就入了英国籍。（admit）

(7) 电影制片人的动机仍然是个谜。（puzzle）

(8) 我的姐姐也在同一班火车上，这纯属巧合。（coincidence）

(9) 无论如何欧洲值得去看一下。（worthwhile）

(10) 他是一位见多识广的值得信赖的旅伴。（trustworthy）

6. Cloze.

Everybody uses the expressions A. M. and P. M. to indicate before noon and after noon. But do you know __(1)__ what they mean，and how these terms __(2)__ into being?

__(3)__ you know，the turning of the earth makes the sun and the stars seem to move __(4)__ the sky. Daylight，of course，begins when the sun rises in the east and ends when it __(5)__ in the west. When the sun is high in the sky，between these two __(6)__ ，half of the daylight hours have been spent.

__(7)__ ，by noticing where the sun stood in the sky，early __(8)__ knew he could tell the time of day. At night，the motion of the stars __(9)__ the same purpose. The important thing __(10)__ keeping time is to know the exact moment of noon. For each of us，__(11)__ we are，noon is when the sun is __(12)__ overhead. Think of an __(13)__ line，a meridian（子午线），drawn across the sky，__(14)__ from the north point of your horizon __(15)__ to the south point.

When the sun __(16)__ your meridian，it is noon for you. While the sun is still __(17)__ of this line or meridian，it is morning. After the sun has crossed this meridian，it is __(18)__ .

The Latin word for "midday" is *meridies*，from which comes our word meridian. __(19)__ A. M. is an abbreviation for ante meridiem，or before midday. P.M is the abbreviation for post medridiem，or after midday.

Each of the world's time zones is about fifteen degrees __(20)__ in longitude（纬度），which is about the same distance the sun moves through the sky in an hour. Everyone who lives in the same time zone observes noon at the same moment. In this way，the time differs by one hour as you move through each time zone.

(1) A. actually   B. basically   C. exactly   D. certainly

(2) A. come   B. have come   C. came   D. had come

(3) A. As   B. If   C. Since   D. Although

(4) A. under   B. toward   C. through   D. across

(5) A. falls   B. drops   C. sets   D. collapses

(6) A. spots   B. positions   C. levels   D. posts

(7) A. However   B. Therefore   C. Furthermore   D. Frequently

(8) A. man	B. woman	C. person	D. child
(9) A. performed	B. acted	C. functioned	D. served
(10) A. at	B. to	C. in	D. of
(11) A. whenever	B. wherever	C. whoever	D. whatever
(12) A. nearly	B. directly	C. obviously	D. especially
(13) A. imagining	B. imaginable	C. imaginative	D. imaginary
(14) A. that stretches	B. to be stretched	C. stretching	D. being stretched
(15) A. down	B. up	C. along	D. through
(16) A. crossed	B. will cross	C. has crossed	D. crosses
(17) A. south	B. east	C. north	D. west
(18) A. night	B. evening	C. noon	D. afternoon
(19) A. So	B. Finally	C. Likewise	D. Yet
(20) A. wide	B. long	C. deep	D. high

Grammar related to Text A

Additional Tasks

Rewrite the following sentences after the models, using *will/shall*+*verb*.
Model:
I promise to keep the secret. → I will keep the secret.
Would you like me to leave now? → Shall I leave now?
(1) I promise to tell him the good news.

(2) I promise to take care of your house when you are away.

(3) I promise not to make the same mistake again.

(4) I promise not to be late for class.

(5) He refuses to pay for the coffee.

(6) This cork refuses to come out.

(7) This mark refuses to come off.

(8) I refuse to answer that question.

(9) Would you like me to start late?

(10) Would it be a good idea for us to discuss that issue next time?

Writing Task | related to Text A

In the space provided for each of the following nine sentences, put the number of the sentence in the order in which it should occur.

____(1)____ Getting your thoughts down on paper is not the final stage of writing a good paragraph or essay.

____(2)____ There remains the rewriting of the first draft so as to shape your idea into a carefully styled composition.

_____ Finally, for smoothness and balance, changes are made between sentences or paragraphs.

_____ A different word may be substituted for the original word because it is easier to understand, is more colorful, gives a more precise meaning, or provides variety.

_____ Ordinarily, editing involves changes at three points: between sentences, within sentences, and in individual words.

_____ At the sentence level, phrases may be put in different order, structures of modification revised, different verb structures selected, or the length of phrases or whole sentences may be altered.

_____ At the word level, spelling and capitalization are checked, but more creatively, words are often changed.

_____ Such changes, designed to clarify relationships between ideas, are often accomplished by punctuating more adequately, by introducing more effective transitional devices, or by restating or removing awkward phrases and sentences.

____(9)____ Editing then — the self-conscious appraisal and revision of your own work — usually makes the difference between a merely acceptable and a truly superior piece of writing.

Text A  Roll Away the Stone

Vocabulary | related to Text A

Additional Tasks

1. **Word Formation.**

   1) Study how the words "wisdom" and "warmth" are formed. Find out the meanings of the suffixes "-dom" and "-th" with the help of a dictionary. Fill in the first blank with the word stem and the second with the suffix.

   wisdom: _____+_____
   warmth: _____+_____

   2) Fill out the table below, changing the given adjectives into nouns by adding the suffix "-dom", and the nouns into adjectives by deleting the suffix.

   Example: wise (*adj.*)+dom → wisdom (*n.*)

adjectives	nouns	adjectives	nouns
free			kingdom
chief			filmdom
beggar			stardom
bachelor			officialdom

   3) Fill out the table below, changing the adjectives into nouns by adding the suffix "-th".
   Example: warm → warmth (*n.*)

adjectives	nouns	adjectives	nouns
strong		wide	
long		broad	
deep			

4) Complete the sentences based on the Chinese given in the brackets.

(1) From childhood，Britney Spears seemed destined for _____ （明星）.

(2) He treated the department like his own private _____ （天下，领域）.

(3) He was praised for his courage，_____ （智慧）and flexibility.

(4) They regained their _____ （自由）after ten years of unjust imprisonment.

(5) The river froze to a _____ （深度）of over a metre.

(6) He showed an astonishing _____ （广度）of learning for one so young.

(7) The needle is seven times smaller than the _____ （宽度）of a human hair.

(8) I've put a T-shirt on under my sweater for extra _____ （暖和）.

(9) He is endowed with a giant's _____ （力气）.

(10) We suffer from too much _____ （官僚作风）.

2. Fill in the blanks with appropriate prepositions or an adverbs from the text.

(1) She's very sensible _____ money.

(2) A suspicion sprang _____ in his mind.

(3) She was not aware _____ what was going on around.

(4) _____ any circumstances a gentleman has no right to hurt a woman.

(5) He was sensible _____ your kindness.

(6) Transactions are _____ a moderate scale.

(7) The Stock Exchange is sensitive _____ political disturbance.

(8) Her interest _____ languages has become deeper than ever.

(9) We based our conclusions _____ facts.

(10) The incident led _____ her resignation.

3. Complete the sentences with the following words and expressions. Use the proper forms.

spring up	compel	in turn	restoration	faith
shape	lift	administer	be absorbed in	take heart

(1) Theory is based on practice and _____ serves practice.

(2) The men _____ from their leader's words.

(3) She felt _____ to accept his invitation.

(4) The company's finances have been badly _____ .

(5) He _____ the reading of Hamlet.

(6) A coolness _____ between them.

(7) The rock is too heavy for me to _____ .

(8) Winning three games _____ their confidence.

(9) He will not steal my money; I have _____ in him.

(10) His attitudes were _____ partly by early experience.

4. **Complete the sentences with the following verbal phrases in their proper forms.**

leave about	leave aside	leave behind	leave off	leave out	leave for

(1) You will not be _____ _____ if you work harder.

(2) They _____ _____ England two days ago.

(3) Mr Newman took up the text where he _____ _____ last week.

(4) They _____ _____ the point on purpose.

(5) Let's _____ the question _____ for a moment.

(6) He was forced to leave the country, _____ _____ his wife and children.

(7) I've decided to _____ _____ eating meat for a while.

(8) He _____ three people _____ the list by mistake.

(9) Don't _____ your books _____ .

(10) We left in a hurry and I must have _____ my keys _____ .

5. **Fill in each blank with one of the two words from each pair and note the difference of meaning between them.**

1) secure   safe

   (1) There is only one _____ way for the cab company to deal with this problem.

   (2) The boys camping in the forest were well protected, and so _____ from harm.

2) sensible   sensitive

   (1) He did not appear to be _____ of the difficulties that lay ahead.

   (2) My mother was very _____ to cold and heat.

3) enough   adequate

   (1) His knowledge of English is _____ for the job, although he is not fluent in the language.

   (2) Enthusiasm alone was not _____ .

6. **Examine the meanings and uses of "find" and "shape" in the sentences below. List other possible ways of using these words, and then make sentences after the models.**

   With so profound a faith in the human heart and its power to grow toward the light, I *find* here reason and cause enough for hope and confidence in the future of mankind. (Para. 4)

   (to find + n.)

In the midst of possible world war, of wholesale destruction, I *find* my only question is this:

(to find + objective clause)

Such faith keeps me continually ready and purposeful with energy to do what one person can toward *shaping* the environment in which the human being can grow with freedom. (Para. 5)

(to shape + *n*.)

(1) I **find** it necessary to get a map.

(2) He **found** himself in a dilemma.

(3) We have to **find** him a job.

(4) I went to the riverbank one day and **found** a crocodile trapped in a net.

(5) We **found** London to be a fantastic city.

(6) Their dream is beginning to take **shape**.

(7) These events have changed the whole **shape** of British politics.

(8) The market is in good **shape**.

(9) We saw a vague **shape** through the mist but we couldn't see who it was.

(10) I get tired easily. I must be out of **shape**.

Other possible uses of "find" and "shape".

find:

shape:

7. **Translate the following into English, using the words and expressions given in the brackets.**
   (1) 健康有助于心神安宁。(administer)
   (2) 他把那个民间故事改写成了叙事诗。(shape)
   (3) 那鞋走路不是很实用。(be sensible for)
   (4) 我们必须终止这种愚蠢的行为。(put an end to)
   (5) 我们克服了许多困难。(overcome)
   (6) 几乎所有体育项目都存在风险。(inherent)
   (7) 她的讲话表现出了她的成熟和人性。(humanity)
   (8) 我们非常喜欢那部电影,认为钱花得很值得。(worth)

8. **Cloze.**

   Many Americans find silence uncomfortable during a buffet or a formal dinner. __(1)__ in the States there is the __(2)__ practice of making "small talk" in certain social situation. Small talk deals __(3)__ various topics, superficially, simply for the sake of keeping a conversation __(4)__ . The topics __(5)__ include the weather, sports, college courses, clothing, food, etc. Small talk is __(6)__ useful at social gathering when you meet someone for the first time, or when polite conversation is expected but no serious discussion ___(7)___.

It is common but not necessarily expected that one should know ___(8)___ in a group before engaging him or her in conversation. ___(9)___, at a party or ___(10)___ informal social gatherings, a simple "May I join you?" and a self-introduction is normally sufficient ___(11)___ acceptance into a group and to join in a conversation. In some ___(12)___, such as the lobby of a concert hall or theater, a waiting room or a classroom, it is common for ___(13)___ to start a conversation even ___(14)___ an introduction.

___(15)___ the informality that pervades U. S. society, people in the States expect those whom they ___(16)___ to put aside ___(17)___ they are doing and listen. As a ___(18)___, the conversation distance between two people is at least two or three ___(19)___. Standing at a closer range will make many Americans feel ___(20)___.

(1) A. But   B. And   C. So   D. Or
(2) A. good   B. bad   C. different   D. widespread
(3) A. with   B. at   C. in   D. out
(4) A. go   B. going   C. goes   D. to go
(5) A. must   B. should   C. might   D. would
(6) A. perhaps   B. hardly   C. widely   D. especially
(7) A. is desired   B. desired   C. desires   D. will desire
(8) A. man   B. someone   C. woman   D. child
(9) A. Otherwise   B. But   C. However   D. Therefore
(10) A. another   B. others   C. any   D. other
(11) A. to gain   B. to give   C. to make   D. to accept
(12) A. rooms   B. places   C. hall   D. house
(13) A. the young   B. the old   C. strangers   D. people
(14) A. with   B. by   C. if   D. without
(15) A. Despite   B. Though   C. As if   D. Because of
(16) A. speak   B. speak to   C. speak at   D. spoke
(17) A. however   B. whenever   C. whatever   D. whoever
(18) A. whole   B. result   C. matter   D. rule
(19) A. feet   B. meters   C. inches   D. miles
(20) A. unease   B. uneasy   C. unequal   D. unfair

> **Grammar** related to Text A

Additional Tasks

1. Combine each pair of the sentences after the model, using *just as*.

Model:

I know that in environments of uncertainty, fear and hunger, the human being is dwarfed and shaped without his being aware of it, *just as* the plant struggling under a stone does not know its own condition. (Para. 2)

(1) In a contest, your opponent is afraid of you.

You are also afraid of him.

(2) The earth revolves around the sun.

The moon travels around the earth.

(3) The computer is replacing the human brain in the repetitive or very rapid tasks of machine operation.

The steam engine has replaced human and animal muscle power.

(4) I'll behave toward them.

I would like to be treated in the same way.

2. **Improve the following sentences.**

(1) Not only the teachers and the students should help each other but they should learn from each other as well.

(2) In no circumstances I would agree to such a proposal.

(3) Hardly I had arrived when I had a new problem to cope with.

(4) So fast he ran that no one could catch up with him.

(5) To such an extent the temperature rose that the firemen had to leave the burning building.

(6) As a diamond is hard, it is quite easy to drill a hole in it with a laser.

Additional Tasks

◁ Writing Task | related to Text A ▷

Combine each pair of sentences. Use the word in the brackets.

(1) It rained heavily this morning.

We went on working. (despite)

(2) Something caused the fire.

It is still a mystery. (what)

(3) He may not be in the library.

I'm not sure about it. (whether)

(4) Take these pills.

You feel sick on the boat. (in case)

(5) You must work harder.

You can pass the exam next month in no other way. (Only ...)

(6) It began to rain.

We had just arrived there. (Hardly ...)

(7) He had just gone to sleep.

The telephone rang again. (no sooner ... than)

(8) You can go out.

You must promise to be back before 9 p. m. (as long as)

Text A 　Winners Never Quit

Vocabulary | related to Text A >

Additional Tasks

1. Word Formation.

1）Study how the word "African" is formed. Find out the meaning of the suffix "-(a)n" with the help of a dictionary. Fill in the first blank with the word stem and the second with the suffix.

African：_____＋_____

2）Fill out the table below，changing the given nouns into adjectives or nouns by adding the suffix "-(a)n".

Example：Europe (*n.*)＋an → European (*adj.*，*n.*)

nouns	adj. /n	nouns	adj. /n
America		Italy	
urb		library	
Asia		technique	
Australia		music	
India		suburb	

3）Complete the Sentences based on the Chinese given in the brackets.

(1) He wants the _____（图书管理员）to show him how to use the library.

(2) The _____（郊区的）areas usually have railroad or bus transportation to neighboring towns.

(3) She is a talented _____（音乐家）as well as is a photographer.

(4) The _____（技术员）is send to measure the hardiness of the material.

(5) In some developing countries more and more people are migrating to _____（城市的）areas.

(6) The difficulty with _____（传记）is that it is partly record and partly art.

(7) The book deals with the reproductive _____（生物）of the buffalo.

(8) You may study medicine or _____（生物化学）.

(9) In the field events the ratio is 75 per cent due to the athlete，15 per cent to the coach and 10 per cent to the _____（生物力学）scientist.

(10) _____（生物医学）research，like everything else in the modem world，is happening faster and faster.

2. **Complete the sentences with the following words and expressions. Use the proper forms.**

be ready to	insist	mount	hang up	break
all of a sudden	rank	show up	anything but	sit up

(1) I had an appointment with him at eight o'clock，but he didn't _____ until nine-thirty.

(2) Let me _____ you _____ in the bed so you'll be more comfortable.

(3) I _____ always _____ work for you.

(4) She's said to be a really very nice lady but she was _____ nice when I met her.

(5) I don't want to be the one to _____ the news to him.

(6) So when did you _____ your boxing gloves/golf clubs/ballet shoes?

(7) _____，the tyre burst.

(8) I _____ that you withdraw your offensive remarks immediately.

(9) He _____ the platform and began to speak to the assembled crowd.

(10) The company commander _____ his soldiers in columns.

3. **Complete the sentences with the following verbal phrases in their proper forms.**

sit down	sit up	sit on	sit out
sit through	sit by	sit back	

(1) The book was so interesting that I _____ all night reading it.

(2) I can't just _____ and watch you waste all our money.

(3) Many people just _____ and do not get concerned about the world's difficulties.

(4) I call him a damned hypocrite and that made him _____.

(5) Dinner's ready! Come and _____.

(6) Don't just _____ idly _____ while other children are busy.

(7) That's a story that _____ somebody _____ straight.

(8) The company has been _____ my letter for weeks without dealing with my complaint.

(9) We had to _____ two hours of speeches.

(10) I'm feeling rather tired, so I think I'll _____ the next dance.

4. **Examine the meanings and uses of "break" and "assume" in the sentences below. List other possible ways of using these words, and then make sentences after the models.**

One hot summer day, the very day before a big swim meet, I decided to *break* the news to my grandma that I was quitting the swim team. (Para. 2)

That day, at age fifteen, I *broke* the national seventeen/eighteen-year-old 400-freestyle record. (Para. 3)

As I sat next to my grandma, I *assumed* my usual position of laying my big head on her tiny little lap so that she could rub it. (Para. 3)

(1) People were throwing stones and several windows **were broken**.

(2) I don't care what your reasons are. The fact is you're **breaking the law**.

(3) Mike claims that his business partner **broke her contract**.

(4) The painting **has broken all records**, selling for over 200 million *yuan*.

(5) The marriage **broke up** just a few years later.

(6) The animals **assumed** their normal resting position.

(7) He finally **assumes** the presidency next week.

(8) This score is **assumed** to represent the achievement of an average 5-year-old.

(9) I think I can safely **assume** that he is not at home.

(10) Jack **assumed** an air of innocence.

Other possible uses of "break" and "assume".

break：

assume：

5. **Translate the following into English, using the words and expressions given in the brackets.**
   (1) 加时赛后,比赛打成 1 比 1 平。(tie)
   (2) 我们生活在一个非常注重舒适的社会里。(rank)
   (3) 这种作法只有好处,毫无害处。(whatsoever)
   (4) 我可以有把握地认定他不在家。(assume)
   (5) 因为家里穷,他不得不辍学。(quit)
   (6) 他很小父母就去世了,是爷爷奶奶把他养大。(raise)
   (7) 他们不敢向她透露噩耗,因为她在生病。(break the news to)
   (8) 他们已经出版了很多论述国际问题的新书。(issue)
   (9) 我要求你立刻收回那些过头的话。(insist)
   (10) 尽管算不上是该地区最便宜的旅游景点,但与其他类似的度假景点相比,它的价位还是很具吸引力的。(competitively)

6. **Cloze.**
   Shopping habits in the United States have changed greatly in the last quarter of the 20th

century. ___(1)___ in the 1900s most American towns and cities had a main street. Main street was always in the heart of a town. This street was ___(2)___ on both sides with many ___(3)___ businesses.

Shoppers walked into stores to look at all sorts of merchandise: clothing, furniture, hardware, and groceries. ___(4)___ some shops offered ___(5)___. These shops included drugstores, restaurants, shoe-repair stores, and barber or hairdressing shop. ___(6)___ in the 1950s, a change began to ___(7)___. Too many automobiles had crowded into main street ___(8)___ too few parking places were ___(9)___ shoppers. Because the streets were crowded, merchants began to look with interest at the open spaces ___(10)___ the city limits. Open space is what their car-driving customers needed. And open space is what they got ___(11)___ the first shopping center was built. Shopping centers ___(12)___ malls started as a collection of small new stores ___(13)___ crowded city centers. ___(14)___ by hundreds of free parking space, customers were drawn away from ___(15)___ areas to outlying malls. And the growing ___(16)___ of shopping centres led ___(17)___ to the building of bigger and better-stocked stores. ___(18)___ the late 1970s, many shopping malls had almost developed into small cities themselves. In addition to providing the ___(19)___ of one-stop shopping, malls were transformed into landscaped parks ___(20)___ benches, fountains, and outdoor entertainment.

(1) A. As early as   B. Early   C. Early as   D. Earlier
(2) A. built   B. designed   C. intended   D. lined
(3) A. varied   B. various   C. sorted   D. mixed-up
(4) A. As well   B. Beside   C. In addition   D. Except that
(5) A. medical care   B. food   C. services   D. cosmetics
(6) A. Suddenly   B. Abruptly   C. Contrarily   D. But
(7) A. took place   B. take place   C. taked place   D. takes place
(8) A. while   B. yet   C. though   D. and then
(9) A. used by   B. available for   C. available to   D. ready for
(10) A. over   B. form   C. out of   D. outside
(11) A. when   B. while   C. since   D. then
(12) A. such as   B. or rather   C. or   D. and
(13) A. out   B. away from   C. next   D. close
(14) A. Attracted   B. Attract   C. Attracting   D. To attract
(15) A. inner   B. central   C. shopping   D. downtown
(16) A. fame   B. distinction   C. popularity   D. liking
(17) A. on   B. in turn   C. by turn   D. in
(18) A. By   B. During   C. In   D. To
(19) A. cheapness   B. convenience   C. readiness   D. handiness
(20) A. because of   B. and   C. with   D. provided

> Grammar | related to Text A >   **Additional Tasks**

1. **Combine each pair of the sentences following the model.**
   Model: The next day we arrived at the swim meet late.

I missed my group of swimmers in the fifteen/sixteen age group. →

The next day we arrived at the swim meet late, missing my group of swimmers in the fifteen/sixteen age group. (Para. 5)

(1) He was drinking coffee.

He listened to the music.

(2) James Watt had never lost faith in himself.

James Watt went on with his experiment.

(3) We walked through the forest.

We found many strange animals.

(4) We looked out of the window of our hotel room.

We saw zigzag mountains.

2. **Complete the sentences with the words in the brackets in their proper forms.**

(1) My coach insisted I _____ (allow) to swim with the next group, the next age older.

(2) I knew she was including me in the race so our long drive _____ (not waste).

(3) I recommended that the student _____ (finish) writing his compositions as soon as possible.

(4) Your advice that she _____ (wait) till next week is reasonable.

 Writing Task | related to Text A >   **Additional Tasks**

Put the following sentences in the right order to form a coherent passage.

(1) The boy was very kind, and he helped the old man to the nearest hospital.

(2) A few days later, the old man died in the hospital, and left all his money to "Mustafa, a local teacher's son who helped me in my hour of need".

(3) Once there was a boy called Ali, a poor fisherman's son.

(4) Of course, because Ali had lied, he did not receive any of the old man's money.

(5) As he was going home one evening, he saw an old man lying by the side of the road, seriously ill.

(6) The old man thanked the boy and asked for his name and address.

(7) The boy was ashamed to admit that his father was a poor fisherman, so he said, "My name is Mustafa and my father is a teacher."

Text A  The Praying Hands

Vocabulary related to Text A

Additional Tasks

1. **Word Formation.**

   1）**Study how the word "triumphant" is formed. Find out the meaning of the suffix "-ant" with the help of a dictionary.**

   triumphant: <u>triumph</u> (*v.*)＋<u>*ant*</u>

   Fill out the table below, changing the given verbs into adjectives by adding the suffix "-ant", and the adjectives into verbs by deleting the suffix.

   Example: vibrate (*n.*) → vibrant (*a.*)

verbs	adjectives	verbs	adjectives
arrogate		lubricate	
buoy			luxuriant
combat			radiant
defy			resultant
hesitate			variant

   2）**Study how the word "enable" is formed. Find out the meaning of the prefix "en-" with the help of a dictionary. Fill in the first blank with the word stem and the second with the prefix.**

   enable：_____＋_____

   Fill out the table below, changing the given adjectives or nouns into verbs by adding the prefix "en-", and the verbs into adjectives or nouns by deleting the prefix.

Example：en＋circle（*n.*）→ encircle（*v.*）

adjectives/nouns	verbs	adjectives/nouns	verbs
cage			enact
courage			encase
large			enrage
slave			enroll
rich			entitle
trust			envision

3）Complete the sentences based on the Chinese given in the brackets.

(1) They are _____（犹豫）about signing a contract.

(2) He is openly _____（反抗的）of the government's policy.

(3) The sun is a _____（发光的）body.

(4) He is intolerably _____（傲慢）.

(5) He has _____（托管）his children to his sister.

(6) Many foreign words and phrases have _____（丰富）the English language.

(7) Many men were _____（征募）during the war.

(8) The balloon _____（膨胀）as we pumped air into it.

(9) The company _____（展望）developing a new market.

(10) She has a pass that _____（给……权利和资格）her to free travel on the railway.

2. Complete the sentences with the following expressions. Use the proper forms.

in appreciation of	by profession	work out	go off to
suffer from	be familiar with	pay homage to	

(1) Finally they _____ a plan for the project.

(2) In the feudal society, all the servants were expected to _____ their lord.

(3) She wrote a poem _____ all the help the doctors and nurses have given her during her illness.

(4) When you first come to a foreign country, you are not _____ the customs there.

(5) He is a doctor _____; he graduated from a medical school and has been working as a doctor for 15 years.

(6) The poor old man cannot see clearly, for he is _____ cataract（白内障）.

(7) I am _____ Vancouver to see my sister.

3. Fill in each blank with one of the two words or phrases from each pair and note the difference of meaning between them.

1) considerate   considerable

   (1) Your children are always very _____ towards old people.

   (2) The city suffered _____ damage as a result of the earthquake.

2) festive   festival

   (1) Our English College will hold a Shakespeare _____ next month.

   (2) On _____ occasions, people will sing, dance and drink to their hearts' content.

3) tribute   contribute

   (1) The pirates demanded _____ from passing ships.

   (2) How much should I _____ to the relief fund?

4) memorable   memorial

   (1) American _____ Day is a tribute to the old soldiers.

   (2) "The Praying Hands" is considered the most _____ work of Albrecht Durer.

5) capacity   capability

   (1) The boy has great _____ in long-distance running.

   (2) That bowl has a _____ of two pints.

4. Complete the sentences with the following verbal phrases in their proper forms.

pass around	pass for	pass by	pass down	pass off
pass off as	pass on	pass over	pass to	pass up

(1) The media has been accused of _____ some of the most disturbing details of the case.

(2) He _____ our house on his way to work.

(3) Take a copy for yourself and _____ the rest _____.

(4) Tales such as these were _____ from generation to generation.

(5) She's fifteen but she could easily _____ eighteen.

(6) The demonstration _____ peacefully.

(7) He then went to the States where he tried to _____ himself _____ an aristocrat.

(8) Could you _____ it _____ to Laura when you finish reading it?

(9) On his aunt's death, all her property will _____ him.

(10) It is a great opportunity — you'd be a fool to _____ it _____.

5. Examine the meanings and uses of "toss" and "abuse" in the sentences below. List other possible ways of using these words, and then make sentences after the models.

They would *toss* a coin. (Para. 2)

Albrecht Durer painstakingly drew his brother's *abused* hands with palms together and thin fingers stretched skyward. (Para. 8)

(1) Let's **toss** to see who should pay the bill.

(2) The ship **tossed** about on the stormy sea.

(3) The children **tossed** the ball to each other.

(4) He **tossed** and turned all night.

(5) As there was only one ticket left, they decided to **toss** up for it.

(6) He **abused** his privileges in activities outside his official capacity.

(7) Help should be provided for the **abused** children.

(8) I ask him not to **abuse** me in private to the newspaper editors.

(9) We **abuse** land because we regard it as a commodity belonging to us.

(10) He has **abused** my confidence in him.

Other possible uses of "toss" and "abuse".

toss：

abuse：

6. **Translate the following into English, using the words and expressions given in the brackets.**

(1) 他的文章散发给了 15 000 名读者。(circulate)

(2) 他道貌岸然。(seemingly)

(3) 这项新发现轰动一时。(sensation)

(4) 她在艺术上追求完美境界。(pursue)

(5) 他要挣很多钱供女儿读完法学院。(finance)

(6) 我花了两个小时才解出这个方程。(work out)

(7) 娇弱的植物必须得到妥善保护以避免风霜的侵袭。(delicate)

(8) 如果他不努力,他永远也不会实现有所成就的抱负。(fulfill)

(9) 她感谢我的帮助。(appreciation)

(10) 医生称赞护士们的工作。(tribute)

7. **Fill in the missing words.**

The age of twenty is just the _____ of life, and one _____ young and _____ of energy. _____, at the same time, a period of life has passed, which makes one sad when he thinks something will _____ come back. It is not silly to feel a certain _____, for when one gets something, he may meanwhile have lost something else. Many things really begin at the _____ of twenty, and certainly all is not over then. One begins to see more and more _____ that life is only a kind of sowing time, and the harvest is still _____ away.

Rewrite the following sentences after the model, using the absolute structure.
Model:

1. **Tears streamed down his pale face, and he sobbed and repeated, over and over, "No ... no ... no ... no."**

   Tears streaming down his pale face, he sobbed and repeated, over and over, "No ... no ... no ... no."

2. **After the experiment had been done, the students went on to write the experiment report.**

   The experiment done, the students went on to write the experiment report.

   (1) Because night enshrouded the earth, nobody could make out what the dark mass was from a distance.

   (2) He lay at full length upon his stomach. His head rested upon his left forearm.

   (3) After my shoes were removed, I entered a low-ceilinged room, treading cautiously on the soft tatami matting.

   (4) While the governor was pondering the matter, more strikers gathered across his path.

   (5) If weather permits, they will go on an outing to the beach tomorrow.

   (6) Since the storm was drawing near, the navy decided to call it a day.

   (7) Because all flights had been cancelled, we decided to take a Greyhound.

   (8) The lecture began, and he left his seat so quietly that no one complained that his leaving disturbed the speaker.

   (9) Darkness set in, and the young people lingered on merrymaking.

   (10) A new technique had been worked out, and the yields as a whole increased by 20 percent.

Rearrange the sentences in the right order and translate them into Chinese.

(1) Some customers want low prices with no inconvenience in purchasing.

(2) Customers have different value of products and services.

(3) It can choose to win through cost, with products of the hottest style and technology, or through intimate relationship with specific customers.

(4) Some others care little about prices, what they care is that the product must represent the hottest style and technology in the market.

(5) Still others require that the products or services satisfy their specific needs.

(6) As a result, if a company wants to be a market leader and keep its edge, it must focus on and excel in one way according to its own condition.

Unit 5

Text A Jules Verne's Trip to the Moon

Additional Tasks

1. **Word Formation.**

   1) Study how the word "bimonthly" is formed. Find out the meaning of the prefix "bi-" with the help of a dictionary and translate the following words into Chinese.

   bimonthly

   biweekly

   bilingual

   bilateral

   bicolor

   binoculars

   2) Study the difference of "employer" and "employee". Find out the meaning of the suffix "-ee" with the help of a dictionary and translate the following words into Chinese.

   addressee

   examinee

   electee

   invitee

   testee

   payee

   trainee

   appointee

   interviewee

3）Complete the sentences based on the Chinese given in the brackets.

(1) With the help of no more than a _____（双筒望远镜）, it is easy to distinguish the two main kinds of lunar landscape.

(2) This journal is a _____（双月刊）, and that one quarterly.

(3) France and Germany have signed a _____（双边的）agreement to help prevent drug smuggling.

(4) In a _____（双语）environment, cross-language references make the students' thinking more sophisticated.

(5) If a _____（学员）is allowed to be sloppy while training, a solid base of sound techniques will not be developed.

(6) If the _____（被邀请的人）will be more than 20 minutes late for an appointment or for a social occasion, it is wise to telephone to say that he or she will be late.

(7) In my research on military revolution, future warfare and national defense development, you are the _____（访谈的对象）whom I most desire to speak with.

(8) Where the _____（收款人）is a fictitious or non-existing person, the bill may be treated as payable to bearer.

(9) If the writer knows the _____（收信人）personally, the first name is used and "With best wishes" may be added.

(10) The new _____（被任命者）will be working closely with both departments.

2. Complete the sentences with the following words and expressions. Use the proper forms.

be headed for	parallel	imaginary	pick up	make up
fantasy	be based on/upon	fascinate	means	chart

(1) Having played hero successfully a thousand times in _____, I never doubted I would do it.

(2) He _____ some excuse about the dog eating his homework.

(3) Anything to do with airplanes and flying _____ him.

(4) The family had no _____ of support.

(5) All the characters in this book are _____.

(6) A wall of rock towered _____ up on one side of the narrow mountain path.

(7) The crew of the sinking tanker _____ by helicopter.

(8) This play _____ a true story.

(9) But for his wound, they'd _____ Texas by now — all of them — but he couldn't ride far and they wouldn't leave him.

(10) On the map we _____ the course of the river.

3. Complete the sentences with the following verbal phrases in their proper forms.

think of	think about	think better of	think through	think twice
think over	think aloud	think on one's feet	think back	think out

(1) She said she needed time to _____ it _____.

(2) I _____ him after I have found out his true motive.

(3) Sorry, I wasn't talking to you. I was just _____.

(4) It was difficult to _____ this maze of contradictory facts and statistics.

(5) A good basketball player can _____.

(6) The photographs made me _____ to my schooldays.

(7) I must _____ before I can promise.

(8) The book is detailed and well _____.

(9) I am _____ purchasing a piano.

(10) I don't care what other people _____ me.

(11) The administration has not really _____ what it plans to do once the fighting stops.

(12) I _____ to the time in 1999 when my father was desperately ill.

4. **Examine the meanings and uses of "parallel" and "chart" in the sentences below. List other possible ways of using these words, and then make sentences after the models.**

Different from the moon travel fantasies before it, Verne's story contains some descriptions that amazingly *parallel* twentieth-century actual moon flights although the idea of man's really going on a trip seemed impossible when Verne wrote his story. (Para. 3)

The Verne men even *charted* the Sea of Tranquility. And the Sea of Tranquility is the place where Neil Armstrong took his "one small step" 104 years later. (Para. 8)

(1) It's a quiet street running **parallel** to the main road.

(2) Cambridge lies near the 52nd **parallel**.

(3) I'm trying to see if there are any obvious **parallels** between the two cases.

(4) It would be easy to draw a **parallel** between the town's history and that of its football club.

(5) **Parallel** experiments are being conducted in Rome, Paris and London.

(6) The events of the last ten days in some ways **parallel** those before the 1978 election.

(7) There is a **chart** on the classroom wall showing the relative heights of all the children.

(8) The sales **chart** shows a distinct decline in the past few months.

(9) We need some sort of graph on which we can **chart** our **progress**.

(10) The map **charts** the course of the river where it splits into two.

Other possible uses of "parallel" and "chart".

parallel:

chart:

5. Translate the following into English, using the words and expressions given in the brackets.

(1) 她非常适合那份工作。(ideal)

(2) 爱因斯坦从小就对各种物理现象和机械现象很入迷。(fascinate)

(3) 就我所知,这是迄今为止下水的最大的一艘轮船。(launch)

(4) 汤姆提议为全家的健康干杯。(toast)

(5) 直升机垂直向上飞起。(vertically)

(6) 整个故事完全是虚构出来的。(make up)

(7) 你的说法跟他告诉我的情况极为相似。(parallel)

(8) 就多数人而言,这一代父母必须把照顾孩子和照顾自己年迈的双亲并重。(in many cases)

(9) 没有幻想和白日梦的一生是严重匮乏的一生。(fantasy)

(10) 这个馆荟萃了来自各个国家各个历史时期的钟表。(amazingly)

6. Cloze.

Among the most popular books being written today are those which are usually classified as science fiction. Hundreds of ___(1)___ are published every year and are read by all kinds of people. ___(2)___, some of the most successful film of recent years have been ___(3)___ on science fiction stories.

It is often thought that science fiction is a ___(4)___ new development in literature, ___(5)___ its ancestors can be found in books written hundreds of years ago. These books were often ___(6)___ with the presentation of some form of an ___(7)___ society, a theme which is ___(8)___ often found in modern-stories.

Most of the classics of science fiction, ___(9)___, have been written within the last one hundred years. Books ___(10)___ writers, such as Jules Verne and H. G. Wells, to ___(11)___ just two well-known authors, have been translated into many languages. ___(12)___ science fiction writers don't write about men from Mars of space adventure stories. They are ___(13)___ interested in predicting the effect of technical progress ___(14)___ society and the human mind; or in ___(15)___ future worlds which are a ___(16)___ of the world ___(17)___ we live in now.

___(18)___ of this their writing has obvious political undertones. In an age when scientific fact frequently ___(19)___ science fiction, the writers may find ___(20)___ difficult to keep ahead of scientific advances.

(1) A. styles   B. titles   C. subjects   D. topics

(2) A. Furthermore B. Otherwise C. Anyway   D. Evidently

(3) A. relied   B. depended C. based   D. focused

(4) A. such   B. quite   C. so   D. fairly

(5) A. as   B. when   C. but   D. if

(6) A. involved B. concerned C. related   D. combined

(7) A. ideal   B. idea   C. identical   D. identified

(8) A. yet   B. still   C. almost   D. already

(9) A. consequently B. therefore C. however   D. moreover

(10) A. by   B. on   C. about   D. for

(11) A. recall   B. mention   C. recommend   D. remind
(12) A. Ancient   B. Former   C. Previous   D. Modern
(13) A. more   B. less   C. never   D. scarcely
(14) A. away   B. on   C. above   D. from
(15) A. recognizing   B. imagining   C. remembering   D. adapting
(16) A. reflection   B. reaction   C. reduction   D. regulation
(17) A. where   B. which   C. there   D. when
(18) A. Despite   B. Instead   C. Because   D. At present
(19) A. reaches   B. attains   C. catches   D. overtakes
(20) A. that   B. this   C. it   D. those

> Grammar   related to Text A

Additional Tasks

1. **Combine each pair of sentences following the model, using _instead of_.**

   Model: The power didn't come from a rocket.

   The power came from a 900-foot cannon drilled vertically into the soil and loaded with 400,000 pounds of gun cotton. →

   The power came from, _instead of_ a rocket, a 900-foot cannon drilled vertically into the soil and loaded with 400,000 pounds of gun cotton.

   (1) I don't want to have an ice cream.
   I want to have a cake.

   (2) I didn't give him money.
   I gave him advice.

   (3) They didn't make a stand.
   They fled.

   (4) Bamboo was not used.
   Paper is used nowadays.

   (5) They must make up their own minds.
   We shouldn't make up their minds for them.

2. **Rewrite the following sentences, reducing clauses to phrases or words.**

   (1) But it comes from a fantasy, which was published in 1865.

   (2) But he did know a great deal about the laws of science, so he wrote an adventure story that was based on them.

(3) The substance, which was discovered almost by accident, has revolutionized medicine.

(4) I hate to see letters that are written in pencil.

(5) We must keep a secret of the things that are being discussed here.

<Writing Task | related to Text A >   **Additional Tasks**

Put the following sentences in the right order to form a coherent passage.

(1) A few nights later the thief did come again, but he did not touch any of the cheap jewelry that Mr. Grey had put out for him.

(2) He therefore bought a camera and fixed it up in his shop so that it would photograph anyone who broke in at night, and put some very cheap jewelry in front of it for the thief.

(3) The police had still not managed to catch the thief three weeks later, so Mr. Grey decided that he would try to do something about it.

(4) Mr. Grey had a nice shop in the main street of a small town.

(5) All went well for some years, and then Mr. Grey's shop was broken into at night twice in one month, and a lot of jewelry was stolen each time.

(6) He took the camera which was worth £150.

(7) He sold jewelry, watches, clocks and other things like those.

Text A  What Is Happiness?

Vocabulary related to Text A

1. **Word Formation.**

1) **Study how the word "waterproof" is formed. Find out the meaning of the suffix "-proof" with the help of a dictionary.**

waterproof: water＋proof

Fill out the table below, changing the given nouns into adjectives by adding the suffix "-proof".

Example: grease (*n.*)＋proof → greaseproof (*a.*)

nouns	adjectives	nouns	adjectives
bullet		dust	
frost		fog	
wind		blood	
fire		sweat	
sound		quake	

2) **Study how the word "subconscious" is formed. Find out the meaning of the prefix "sub-" with the help of a dictionary.**

subconscious: sub＋conscious

Fill out the table below, changing the given nouns into nouns that begin with the prefix "sub-".

Example: sub+division ($n.$) → subdivision ($n.$)

nouns	nouns	nouns	nouns
culture		continent	
soil		surface	
structure		tropics	
system		group	
title		way	

3) Complete the sentences based on the Chinese given in the brackets.

(1) "_____"（次大陆）is often used to refer to the area that contains India，Pakistan，and Bangladesh.

(2) In order to avoid disturbing his neighbors when he practised the piano，he used _____（隔声的）material to decorate his windows.

(3) These herbs send their roots right down into the _____（下层土，底土）.

(4) Police usually wear _____（防弹）vest to protect themselves.

(5) A _____（亚文化群）refers to the ideas，art，and way of life of a group of people within a society who have different ideas，art，etc. from the rest of that society.

(6) More and more people in Shanghai take the _____（地铁）to work.

(7) Tom invented a new type of _____（防风）umbrella which sells very well at the market.

(8) The have finished a _____（地下）nuclear test.

(9) The stables were all _____（防火性能的）.

(10) He had to wear a pair of _____（防水的）trousers to do the experiment in the deep water.

2. Complete the sentences with the following expressions. Use the proper forms.

free of	all the same	call upon	satisfy one's desire
run out of	speak of	take pains	deal with

(1) She would have to _____ all her strength if she was to survive the next few months.

(2) We've _____ paper for the photocopier.

(3) He needed to _____ for revenge.

(4) It rained every day of our holiday — but we had a good time _____.

(5) The whole robbery _____ inside knowledge on the part of the criminals.

(6) She'll never be completely _____ the disease.

(7) I _____ to select the best staff available.

(8) She's used to _____ difficult customers.

3. **Complete the following pairs of sentences with the correct word.**

   1) industrial   industrious

      (1) Germany is considered to be an _____ country.

      (2) The Chinese people are brave and _____ .

   2) considerable   considerate

      (1) It was _____ of you not to play the piano while I was having a sleep.

      (2) When her father died, Jane became head of a _____ business empire.

   3) practicable   practical

      (1) Now you are going to live in France, you will be able to make _____ use of your knowledge of French.

      (2) Is it _____ to try to grow crops in deserts?

   4) sensitive   sensational

      (1) It was a _____ news report.

      (2) The old woman is very weak and _____ to cold.

   5) historical   historic

      (1) Where did the _____ May 4th Movement take place?

      (2) Is this a _____ novel?

4. **Complete the sentences with the following verbal phrases in their proper forms.**

get about	get after	get across	get along	get around
get behind	get down	get down to	get through	get up

   (1) I tried phoning her earlier, but I couldn't _____ .

   (2) So you've just come back from Japan and now you're off to Canada? You _____ a bit, don't you?

   (3) Vicky and Ellen seem to be _____ much better these days.

   (4) They _____ with the house payments when the interest rates went up.

   (5) This is the message that we want to _____ to the public.

   (6) It's time you _____ looking for a job.

   (7) Word (= the news) _____ that Jeanette and Dave were having an affair.

   (8) I'm not going to _____ on my knees and beg him to come.

   (9) The whole audience _____ and started clapping.

   (10) _____ Shirley and tell her not to wait for us.

5. **Examine the meanings and uses of "pursue" and "demand" in the sentences below. List other possible ways of using these words, and then make sentences after the models.**

The right to *pursue* happiness is issued to us all with our birth, but no one seems quite sure what it is. (Para. 1)

We *demand* it because without difficulty there can be no game. (Para. 6)

(1) He was killed by the driver of a stolen car who was being hotly **pursued** by the police.

(2) The company has been **pursuing** Holton for some time, but so far he has rejected all their offers.

(3) The press has **pursued** this story relentlessly.

(4) He's been **pursuing** her for months and yet she's so clearly not interested.

(5) We need to decide soon what marketing strategy we should **pursue** for these new products.

(6) He has always **demanded** the highest standards of behaviour from his children.

(7) He seems to lack many of the qualities **demanded** of a successful politician.

(8) The government is unlikely to agree to the rebels' **demands** for independence.

(9) Good teachers are always in (great) **demand**.

(10) The **demands** of nursing are too great for a lot of people.

Other possible uses of "pursue" and "demand".

pursue：

demand：

6. **Translate the following into English, using the words given in the brackets.**

(1) 我们生活在一个完全是人工造就的环境里。(man-made)

(2) 这份契约本来肯定会使他破产的。(ruin)

(3) 有些家长在收养问题上争论不休。(issue)

(4) 就在那一刻他的沉思被人打破了。(contemplation)

(5) 救援的人到达时,幸存者已饿坏了。(starve)

(6) 这事只会给那个小小的社区带来无穷无尽的苦难。(everlasting)

(7) 他们生活在一个阴暗、秘密的世界里,缺少与人交往的信心。(lack)

(8) 他以经营古式家具为业。(dealer)

(9) 你认为圣经是一部有关上帝的书吗?(holy)

(10) 他喜欢莫扎特的带有浓厚宗教气息的音乐。(religious)

7. **Cloze.**

It is difficult to imagine what life would be like without memory. The meaning of thousands of everyday perceptions, the bases of the decisions we make, and the roots of our habits and skills are to be ___(1)___ in our past experiences, which are brought into the present ___(2)___ memory.

Memory can be defined as the capacity to keep ___(3)___ available for later use. It includes not only "remembering" things like arithmetic or historical facts, but also any change in the way an animal typically behaves. Memory is ___(4)___ when a rat gives up eating grains because he has sniffed something suspicious in the grain pile.

Memory ___(5)___ not only in human and animals but also in some physical objects and machines. Computers, for example, contain devices for ___(6)___ data for later use. It is interesting to compare the memory storage capacity of a computer ___(7)___ that of a human beings. The instant access memory of a large computer may hold up to 100,000 "words" ready for ___(8)___ use. An average American teenager probably recognizes the meanings of about 100,000 words of English. However, this is but a fraction of the total ___(9)___ of information which the teenager has stored. Consider, for example, the number of facts and places that the teenager can recognize on sight. The use of words is the basis of the advanced problems solving intelligence of human beings. A large part of a person's memory is in terms of words and ___(10)___ of words.

(1) A. found   B. kept   C. sought   D. predicted
(2) A. by   B. from   C. with   D. in
(3) A. experiences B. bases   C. observations D. information
(4) A. called   B. taken   C. involved   D. introduced
(5) A. exists   B. appears   C. affects   D. seems
(6) A. storing   B. containing   C. maintaining   D. restoring
(7) A. to   B. with   C. against   D. for
(8) A. progressive B. instructive   C. instant   D. protective
(9) A. deal   B. number   C. mount   D. amount
(10) A. combinations B. corrections C. coordination D. collections

Grammar   related to Text A   **Additional Tasks**

Provide the correct words to make comparisons.
Model:
1. _____ _____ you argue with him, _____ _____ notice he takes.
   The more you argue with him, the less notice he takes.
2. _____ _____ the temperature, _____ _____ the liquid evaporates.
   The higher the temperature, the faster the liquid evaporates.
   (1) _____ _____ I see of him, _____ _____ I like him.
   (2) _____ _____ we do for the people, _____ _____ we feel.
   (3) _____ _____ he tried, _____ _____ progress he seemed to make.

(4) _____ _____ wit a man has, _____ _____ he knows that he wants it.

(5) _____ _____ tickets you can sell, _____ _____ .

(6) _____ _____ north you go, _____ _____ severe the winters are.

(7) _____ _____ the teacher talked, _____ _____ I understood.

(8) _____ _____ you start, _____ _____ quickly you'll finish.

(9) We'll have to begin our journey early tomorrow; in fact, _____ _____ , _____

_____ .

(10) _____ _____ the velocity of steam, _____ _____ the turbine speed.

Writing Task | related to Text A >

Additional Tasks

In the space provided for each of the following nine sentences, put the number of the sentence in the order in which it should occur.

_(1)_ A jet engine works with only three basic parts: an air intake, a combustion chamber, and an exhaust outlet.

_____ Air and fuel mixed in the combustion chamber catch fire.

_____ First, air comes in through the air intake.

_____ The hot exploding gases push out at great speed through the exhaust outlet.

_____ The air and fuel mixture actually explodes in the chamber.

_____ As the gases push outward and backward, the plane moves forward.

Text A  Disc Jockey

Vocabulary related to Text A

Additional Tasks

1. **Word Formation.**

   1）Study how the word "aged" is formed. Find out the meaning of the suffix "-ed" with the help of a dictionary.

   aged：age＋ed

   Fill out the table below, changing the given nouns into adjectives by adding the suffix "-ed", and the adjectives into nouns by deleting the suffix.

   Example：talent → talented

nouns	adjectives	nouns	adjectives
beard			colored
culture			concerned
conceit			haired
gift			ringed
wood			wounded

   2）Study how the word "surname" is formed. Find out the meaning of the prefix "sur-" with the help of a dictionary.

   surpass：sur＋name

   Add prefix "sur-"to the following words or vice versa. Pay attention to the change of the meaning of the new words.

charge			surpass
face			surreal
mount			surround
plus			surtax

3) **Complete the sentences based on the Chinese given in the brackets.**

(1) He is so _____（自负）. He always holds an unduly high opinion of himself.

(2) She is a _____（有天赋的）child，quick to learn everything.

(3) There is a _____（绿树成荫）area near the highway.

(4) Many _____（有色的）people live in the slums near the Main Street.

(5) I am very _____（牵挂）about her.

(6) The table had a shiny _____（表面），but underneath it was dull and rough.

(7) The church steeple _____（高于）the square.

(8) The fence _____（围绕）the school.

(9) If you order something not included in the meal，there is a _____（额外付费）.

(10) The later comers _____（超过）the early starters.

2. **Complete the sentences with the following expressions. Use the proper forms.**

take on	take a back seat	spring up	apply to
at the expense of	brighten up	in time	

(1) Her presence greatly _____ the evening party.

(2) The principle of diligence and frugality _____ all undertakings.

(3) She declined to travel _____ of her company and paid for the trip herself.

(4) Newly opened markets have _____ on the outskirts of the city.

(5) You are a newcomer here. But _____ you will learn everything.

(6) Her voice _____ a troubled tone.

(7) With the advent of air-conditioners，fans _____ a back seat now.

3. **Fill in each blank with one of the two words or phrases from each pair and note the difference of meaning between them.**

1) award   reward

(1) The police have offered a large _____ for information leading to the robber's arrest.

(2) The Academy _____ is held every year.

2) regretful   regrettable

(1) There has been a _____ lack of communication between the union and the

management.

(2) I felt rather _____ that the affair ended like that.

3) successive   successful

(1) She has been talking for three _____ hours.

(2) The _____ surgical operation won the doctor high reputation.

4) sensible   sensitive

(1) If you are _____ you will study for another year.

(2) She is _____ to what people think of her.

5) rise   arise

(1) The river _____ every spring.

(2) A new spirit of freedom was _____ .

4. Complete the sentences with the following verbal phrases in their proper forms.

call away	call in	call off	call over	call forth
call out for	call out	call upon	call for	call up

(1) Do you mind if we just _____ at the supermarket?

(2) His remarks _____ a storm of protest.

(3) Paul wasn't at the meeting. He was _____ on urgent business, apparently.

(4) The match had to be _____ because of the freezing weather.

(5) The army is in a state of readiness in case it should be _____ to launch an offensive.

(6) Someone in the crowd _____ his name, but he couldn't see who it was.

(7) I don't want to cook tonight. Should I _____ a pizza?

(8) It's the sort of work that _____ a high level of concentration.

(9) You can _____ and leave a message if I'm out.

5. Examine the meanings and uses of "improve" and "spread" in the sentences below. List other possible ways of using these words, and then make sentences after the models.

Communications *improved*. (Para. 2)

Because the term, "disc jockey" has *spread* across the country. (Para. 7)

(1) The government will have to **improve** its image if it wants to win support from the public.

(2) Time is so precious. You should **improve** your leisure by studying.

(3) He came back from his holiday with greatly **improved** health.

(4) I am unable to **improve** on his suggestion.

(5) Today life has vastly **improved.**

(6) Father **spread** the world map out flat on the floor and tried to find out the town where his son was fighting.

(7) She **spread** the bread with butter.

(8) The fire **spread** from the factory to the houses nearby.

(9) It is a big project. We have to **spread** the cost over three years.

(10) We see a vast field **spread** with wild flowers.

Other possible uses of "improve" and "spread".

improve：

spread：

6. **Translate the following into English, using the words and expressions given in the brackets.**
   (1) 数以千计的新企业在过去的几年里纷纷涌现出来。(spring up)
   (2) 她拉上窗帘，把灯打开。(turn on)
   (3) 无疑我们将最终获胜。(doubt)
   (4) 由于该政党的政策不得人心，许多人都投了反对票。(opposing)
   (5) 他完成了工作，但却牺牲了健康。(at the expense of)
   (6) 热情的女主人用美味的茶点和美妙的音乐招待客人们。(entertain)
   (7) 交易会上他们公司的产品因缺乏创新而很少有人问津。(take a back seat)
   (8) 她把毛巾在沙滩上铺开然后躺下来。(spread out)
   (9) 老师们指导他通过了考试。(steer)
   (10) 这项规定只适用于大学一年级学生。(apply to)

7. **Fill in the missing words.**

   Every people has its own ___(1)___ of saying things, its own special expressions. Many everyday American expressions are ___(2)___ on colors.

   Red is a hot color. Americans often use it to ___(3)___ heat. They may say they are ***red hot*** about something unfair. When they are red hot they are very ___(4)___ about something. The small hot tasting peppers found in many Mexican foods are called red hots ___(5)___ their color and their fiery taste. Fast loud music is popular ___(6)___ many people. They may say the music is red hot，especially the kind ___(7)___ Dixieland jazz.

   Blue is a ___(8)___ color. The traditional **blues music** in the United States is the opposite of red hot music. Blues is slow，___(9)___ and soulful. Duke Ellington and his orchestra recorded a famous song — Mood Indigo — about the deep blue color, indigo. In the words of the song："You ain't been blue till you've had that Mood Indigo." Someone who is ___(10)___ is very sad.

◁ **Grammar** | related to Text A ▷   **Additional Tasks**

Fill in the blanks with *whatever*, *whichever*, *whoever*, *whosever*, *whenever*, *wherever*, *however*, *whomever*.

Model：... for many believed that *whatever* the disc jockeys played was good. (Para. 5)

(1) We can assign the task to _____ is capable and trustworthy.

(2) _____ tough the task is, he always tries his best to complete it on time.

(3) Give out the gift to _____ you meet on the road.

(4) _____ the bag is, I will take it away, for it just stands in the way.

(5) All those skirts are beautiful. You can pick _____ style you like.

(6) Come and see me _____ it is convenient to you.

(7) _____ anything happens in the world, reporters are on the spot to report the news.

(8) The government has promised to do _____ lies in its power to ease the hardships of the victims in the flood-stricken area.

| Writing Task | related to Text A | **Additional Tasks** |

Rearrange the sentence order and translate them into Chinese.

(1) And a passenger on a boat who is feeling very sick from high waves may **look very green**.

(2) A person who has a sick feeling stomach may say she feels a little **green**.

(3) The color green is natural for trees and grass.

(4) But it is an unnatural color for humans.

(5) Some people are green with envy because a friend has more dollars or **greenbacks**.

(6) Dollars are called greenbacks because that is the color of the back side of the paper money.

(7) That person may say he is **green with envy**.

(8) Sometimes a person may be upset because he does not have something as nice as a friend has, like a fast new car.

Text A  What's Your Spiritual IQ?

Vocabulary   related to Text A

Additional Tasks

1. Word Formation.

1） Study how the word "maltreat" is formed. Find out the meaning of the prefix "mal-" with the help of a dictionary and translate the following words into Chinese.

maltreat：＿＿＿＿＋＿＿＿＿

malpractice	malnutrition
malfunction	maladministration
malformation	maladjustment
malcontent	

2） Fill in the table below, changing the given verbs into nouns by adding the suffix "-ant" or "-ent".

Example： apply（*v.*）→ applicant（*n.*）

verbs	nouns	verbs	nouns
correspond		study	
resist		depend	
participate		digest	
serve		preside	
excite		assist	
reside			

3）Complete the sentences based on the Chinese given in the brackets.

(1) Some of the keys on the keyboard have started to _____ （出现故障）.

(2) All the trouble is being caused by a handful of _____ （不满分子）.

(3) Thousands of refugees are dying because of the incompetence and _____ （管理不当） of local officials.

(4) Regular daydreaming was regarded as evidence of _____ （不适应环境） or an escape from life's realities and responsibilities.

(5) Qi Baishi's paintings have won great favor among the Chinese people because he reflected their national sentiments and criticized _____ （时弊）.

(6) I was an active _____ （参加） of academic，sports，and recreational activities.

(7) The patient has become _____ （抵抗力） to certain medicines.

(8) He worked as an _____ （助理） to the President.

(9) Her father's pension will provide for his _____ （受抚养者）.

(10) The writer of the book is a _____ （记者） with an army （＝a war correspondent） （随军记者）.

2. Complete the sentences with the following words and expressions. Use the proper forms.

cultivate	savor	nudge	pop into	tuned in
turn down	focus on	sign up	tear into	perspective

(1) I _____ him awake，but he drifted off again.

(2) She just doesn't seem to be _____ to her students' needs.

(3) I've just got to _____ the bank to get some money.

(4) It was the first chocolate he'd tasted for over a year，so he _____ every mouthful.

(5) Unfortunately，if he doesn't agree with you, he tends to _____ you.

(6) _____ the air conditioner，will you?

(7) They searched for a place where they could live in _____ .

(8) We should learn to view an issue from a historical _____ .

(9) She's _____ for evening classes at the community college.

(10) Tonight's programme _____ the way that homelessness affects the young.

3. Fill in each blank with one of the two words from each pair in its proper form and note the difference of meaning between.

1) gaze   peer

(1) _____ through the key hole，he found a fang of three talking mysteriously in the room.

(2) She _____ sadly after the ship until it disappeared in the darkness.

2) capacity   capability

(1) He has the _____ for great achievement.

(2) As a scientist, he has the _____ of doing important research.

3) **solitude   isolation**

    (1) The criminals kept the kidnapped child in _____ by removing him to a deserted farmhouse.

    (2) The lighthouse keeper, in his wild _____, almost forgets the common language of men.

4. Complete the sentences with the following verbal phrases in their proper forms.

show up   show (a) round   show off   show over   show out

(1) To my surprise, she failed to _____ _____.

(2) A guide _____ us _____ the exhibition.

(3) I wish you wouldn't _____ me _____ in front of my parents by getting so drunk.

(4) She likes to wear short skirts to _____ _____ her legs.

(5) Please _____ this gentleman _____.

(6) After lunch the VIPs will be _____ _____ the new Arts Centre.

(7) She only bought that sports car to _____ _____ and prove she could afford one.

(8) We were expecting thirty people to come, but half of them never _____ _____.

(9) Let me know when you're coming to Cambridge and I'll _____ you _____.

(10) She likes to _____ people _____ in public.

5. Examine the meanings and uses of "while" and "reflect" in the sentences below. List other possible ways of using these words, and then make sentences after the models.

While we're all born with SQ, most of us aren't even aware that we have it. (Para. 5)

While most of us rely on gut feelings to alert us to danger, spiritual intelligence usually nudges us, not away from, but toward some action that will lead to a greater good. (Para. 12)

In the car, instead of reaching for the radio dial, use the time to *reflect*. (Para. 6)

(1) You were there quite a **while**, weren't you?

(2) I thought I heard him come in **while** we were having dinner.

(3) **While** I accept that he's not perfect in many respects, I do actually quite like the man.

(4) Tom is very extrovert and confident **while** Katy's shy and quiet.

(5) He saw himself **reflected** in the water/mirror/shop window.

(6) The statistics **reflect** a change in people's spending habits.

(7) She **reflected** that this was probably the last time she would see him.

(8) When one player behaves disgracefully, it **reflects** (badly) on the whole team.

Other possible uses of "while" and "reflect".

while：

reflect：

6. **Translate the following into English，using the words and expressions given in the brackets.**

（1）在艰难的时势下，没有别的法子，你只能憋着一口气干下去，尽自己的最大努力。（take a deep breath）

（2）我们之间唯以友谊为重，不将自己的信仰强加于人。（focus on）

（3）她报名参加了红十字会举办的护理基础速成班的学习。（sign up）

（4）中国的快速增长和崛起，将提高汉语的重要性，而我们掌握汉语将使我们能够进入这个苗壮的经济体。（tap into）

（5）他本想狠狠地训我一顿，但是现在是琼斯在问话，而琼斯又不愿让别人打搅。（tear into）

（6）我叔叔一时冲动买下了那房子。（impulse）

（7）他拥抱她，接着递给她一束玫瑰花。（bouquet）

（8）我努力试图对我周围发生的事情进行思考。（reflect）

（9）由于地理位置不同，德国和英国对东欧局势持有不同观点。（perspective）

（10）我们总是在 10 点钟收听新闻。（tune in to）

7. **Cloze.**

　　Every country has its own ___(1)___ dining customs. Americans ___(2)___ the first rule of being a polite guest is to be on time. If a person is invited to dinner at six-thirty, the hostess expects him ___(3)___ at six-thirty or ___(4)___ a few minutes after. Because she usually does the cooking，she times the meal so that the hot rolls and the coffee and the meat will be ___(5)___ at the time the guests come. If they are late, the food will not be so good, ___(6)___ the hostess will be disappointed. ___(7)___ the guest cannot come on time，he calls his host or hostess on the telephone，gives the reason，and tells ___(8)___ what time he can come. ___(9)___ the situation, guests sometimes bring a box of candy or some flowers to give to the hostess as a ___(10)___ of appreciation.

　　As guests continue to arrive, it is usually considered ___(11)___ for the men in the group to ___(12)___ when a woman enters the room and continue to stand until she is seated. ___(13)___, most young people and some groups of older people ___(14)___ stress equality of the sexes no longer observe the custom. A visitor should be ___(15)___ to each situation and follow the lead of the Americans present.

　　When the guests sit down at a dinner table, it is a ___(16)___ for the men to help the ladies by pushing their chairs under them. Some Americans ___(17)___ do this, so the visitors must notice what others do and do ___(18)___. ___(19)___ the meal is under way, if the dinner is in a private home, a guest ___(20)___ embarrassment by leaving the talk to someone else.

（1）A. peculiar　　　　B. usual　　　　C. strange　　　　D. rather

（2）A. think that　　　B. feels that　　C. regard　　　　 D. feel that

（3）A. being there　　 B. to be there　　C. to there　　　　D. be there

(4) A. less not than	B. at least	C. not more than	D. more than
(5) A. for the best	B. at their best	C. at best	D. in one's best
(6) A. however	B. but	C. and	D. this
(7) A. When	B. While	C. Unless	D. Until
(8) A. in	B. on	C. at	D. within
(9) A. Depend on	B. Depending on	C. Depended on	D. Dependence
(10) A. sign	B. signal	C. mark	D. expression
(11) A. politely	B. polite	C. politeness	D. impolite
(12) A. sit	B. laugh	C. stand	D. cry
(13) A. Moreover	B. Therefore	C. Thus	D. However
(14) A. that	B. which	C. whom	D. whose
(15) A. sensible	B. sensitive	C. senseless	D. sense
(16) A. habit	B. custom	C. way	D. customary
(17) A. not do	B. no longer	C. may	D. will
(18) A. same	B. alike	C. like	D. likewise
(19) A. Unless	B. If	C. Until	D. When
(20) A. may avoid	B. can avoid	C. must avoid	D. should avoid

Additional Tasks

Grammar | related to Text A

1. **Combine each pair of simple sentences by means of subordination.**

Model: This is our house. We bought the house last month.

→ This is the house we bought last month.

(1) My father prepared the dinner yesterday.
I had my dinner.

(2) The children came to the zoo.
They liked the monkeys best.

(3) They need more help in Chinese.
That is quite obvious.

(4) Most of the buses were already full.
The buses were surrounded by the crowd.

(5) Mathematicians have found that even using the latest electronic equipment they would have to build a 10,000-kilo computer.
The mathematicians have tried to copy the way the brain works.

2. **Improve the following sentences.**

(1) That's a pity that she didn't get some sensible advice at the beginning.

(2) Most women think it is unfair why they do not earn equal pay for equal work.

(3) Due to the refraction of light rays, this is impossible for the naked eyes to determine the exact location of a star close to the horizon.

(4) He spoke English so well that he was taken for granted that he was a native speaker.

(5) I feel it a great honor having been asked to speak before such a large audience.

(6) Rarely he completes his assignment on time.

(7) Nowhere in the city I have seen such beautiful parks in Shanghai.

(8) Not until recently scientists knew much about that disease.

Writing Task | related to Text A

Additional Tasks

Put the following sentences in each group in the right order to form a coherent passage.

(1) And if you have the opportunity to live in another culture, the experience will show you many things, above all, about your own culture.

(2) It will offer you a look at cultures from every part of the earth.

(3) In addition, the experience can also show you a great deal about your own personal beliefs, attitudes, and perceptions.

(4) Being able to communicate in another language will open doors for you to experience a world of new people, places, and ideas.

(5) Within a short time in another culture, you will find that you begin to learn a great deal about yourself and your own country and culture.

(6) Learning to communicate in another language may be very difficult and frustrating at times, but it can also be one of the most rewarding experiences of your life.

(7) It will reveal cultural similarities and differences that you had never noticed in the past.

Text A  Whitewashing Aunt Polly's Fence

Vocabulary related to Text A

Additional Tasks

1. Word Formation.

1) Study how the word "cooperate" is formed. Find out the meaning of the prefix "co-" with the help of a dictionary.

cooperate: co+operate

Add prefix "co-" to the following words or vice versa. Pay attention to the change of meaning of the new words. Add more words to the list.

Example: star → costar

author			coeducation
exist			cohabitation
founder			coownership
relate			correspond
incidence			cosponsor

2) Study how the word "childlike" is formed. Find out the meaning of the suffix "-like" with the help of a dictionary.

childlike: child+ *like*

Fill out the table below, changing the given nouns into adjectives by adding the suffix "-like", and adjectives into nouns by deleting the suffix.

Example：lady＋like：ladylike

nouns	adjectives	nouns	adjectives
business			catlike
clock			hairlike
flower			silklike
gentleman			sportsmanlike
wave			winglike

3）Complete the sentences based on the Chinese given in the brackets.

（1）Two strains of philosophy _____（共同存在）in each of his major works.

（2）Her account of the incident _____（和……相一致）with his.

（3）This book is _____（合著）by two famous professors.

（4）The two great powers _____（并存）for many years.

（5）It was no _____（巧合）that the two disappeared on the same day.

（6）He was good-looking and _____（有绅士风度），he had a pleasant countenance，and easy，unaffected manners.

（7）No winter marred（损坏）his face or stained his _____（如花般的）bloom.

（8）All radiant energy has _____（波浪状的）characteristics，analogous to（类似于）those of waves that move through water.

（9）Negotiations were conducted in a _____（公事公办的）manner.

（10）Tropical marine fishes have enlarged _____（如翅膀似的）fins used for brief gliding flight.

2. Restate the sentences，replacing the underlined parts with expressions from the text.

（1）He is making himself a laughing stock in the classroom. All the students are <u>laughing at</u> him.

（2）When the film star stepped onto the stage，she waved her hands to the audience <u>now and then</u>.

（3）Don't <u>stop halfway</u>；otherwise you cannot reap the final glory.

（4）That naughty boy is fidgeting <u>all the time</u>.

（5）We have <u>used up</u> all the money.

（6）You should <u>give thought and consideration to</u> the instruction.

3. Complete the sentences with the following verbal phrases in their proper forms.

do away with	do down	do for	do in	do out
do ... out of	do over	do up	do with	do without

(1) There is no milk left, so I'm afraid you'll just have to _____.

(2) They are getting some new appliances and want to _____ their kitchen at the same time.

(3) It seemed that everyone at the meeting was trying to _____ her _____.

(4) Driving on rough roads has really _____ my car.

(5) These ridiculous rules and regulations should have been _____ years ago.

(6) She always _____ her presents _____ beautifully in golden paper.

(7) When we got back home, we were completely _____.

(8) I'm sure she won't know what to _____ herself when the kids leave home.

(9) Jane was convinced that he was trying to _____ her _____ her inheritance.

(10) I'm off work next week, so I'm going to _____ the kids' rooms.

4. **Examine the meanings and uses of "pay" and "allow" in the sentences below. List other possible ways of using these words, and then make sentences after the models.**

Perhaps he could find some way to *pay* someone to paint the fence. (Para. 2)

Each one came along the street, stopped to laugh, but soon begged to be *allowed* to paint. (Para. 23)

(1) He **paid** three dollars for a hamburger.

(2) All the employees are required to **pay** taxes.

(3) I'll **pay** him back for his insults.

(4) She **paid** the price for her unpopular opinions.

(5) It doesn't **pay** to get angry.

(6) We **allow** smoking only in restricted areas.

(7) No pets are **allowed** inside.

(8) The schedule **allows** time for a coffee break.

(9) This money **allows** me to buy a car.

(10) It takes about two hours to get to their office building, **allowing** for possible traffic delays.

Other possible uses of "pay" and "allow".

pay：

allow：

5. **Translate the following into English, using the words and expressions given in the brackets.**

(1) 她将炸圈饼放入咖啡。(dip)

(2) 走进树林你能听到鸟儿悦耳的歌声。(melodious)

(3) 他退后几步审视自己的作品。(survey)

(4) 到达山顶时,她浑身是汗。(sweat)

(5) 雨滴滴嗒嗒下了两周,多么阴沉的天气。(depressing)

(6) 雷雅科卡(Leo Ioacoco)终于当上了福特汽车公司的总裁。(attain)

(7) 他一贫如洗,家里只有几件破烂家具。(bits of)

(8) 厨房飘来的香味使我垂涎三尺。(water)

(9) 两人成伴,三人不欢。(company)

(10) 价格已间接做了调整。(from time to time)

6. Fill in the missing words.

Samuel Langhorne Clemens, better known by the ___(1)___ name of Mark Twain, was the first real American author to come from country west of Mississippi River. He was born in Florida, Missouri on November 30, 1835. His ___(2)___ was spent in the town of Hannibal, Missouri. Clemens' father died when the boy was twelve years old, and he went to work in his brother's print shop ___(3)___ the next six years. At the age of eighteen he ___(4)___ out to see the world, ___(5)___ as a job printer in Saint Louis, Chicago, New York, Philadelphia, and other places. In 1857 he was ___(6)___ by the lure of the river life of the Mississippi, and ___(7)___ a steamboat pilot. It is ___(8)___ this work that he got the idea of his pen name, "Mark Twain". It was a nautical term ___(9)___ by sailors to report soundings to the ship's officers. One of Clemem's best books, *Life on the Mississippi*, is built ___(10)___ his experiences around his time.

◀ Grammar | related to Text A ▷   **Additional Tasks**

Choose the answer that best completes each of the following sentences, paying attention to the usage of Subjunctive Mood.

Model:

If he *hadn't run out of* whitewash, he *would have owned* everything belonging to the boys in the village. (Para. 24)

(1) _____ if I had arrived yesterday without letting you know beforehand?

    A. Would you be surprised   B. Were you surprised

    C. Had you been surprised   D. Would you have been surprised

(2) All of us would have enjoyed the party much more if there _____ such a crowd of people there.

    A. weren't   B. hasn't been

    C. hadn't been   D. wouldn't be

(3) I was to have made a speech if _____.

    A. I was not called away   B. nobody would have called me away

    C. I had not been called away   D. nobody called me away

(4) _____ , the crops would be saved.

    A. If it rained   B. If it would rain

    C. Should it rain   D. Would it rain

(5) _____ , he would not have recovered so quickly.

    A. Hadn't he been taken good care of   B. Had he not been taken good care of

    C. He had not been taken good care of   D. Had he been taken good care of

(6) _____ you were busy, I wouldn't have bothered you with my questions.

    A. If I realized   B. Had I realized

    C. I realized that a   D. As I realized

(7) If you _____ in such a hurry, you _____ sugar into the sauce instead of salt.

    A. were not, would   B. were, would put

    C. had been, would have put   D. had not been, would not have put

(8) _____ for the fact that she broke her leg, she might have passed the exam.

    A. Had it not been   B. Hadn't it been

    C. Was it not   D. Were it not

(9) _____ your timely advice, I would never have known how to go about the work.

    A. Unless   B. But for

    C. Except for   D. Not for

(10) _____ their help, we would not have succeeded.

    A. Hadn't been for   B. Had it not been for

    C. It hadn't been for   D. Had not it been for

Additional Tasks

◁ Writing Task | related to Text A ▷

Rearrange the sentence order and translate them into Chinese.

(1) Suddenly, I heard a noise up the river.

(2) They were looking for my body in the river.

(3) I was warm and comfortable and I didn't want to get up.

(4) There was Pop, Judge Thatcher, Tom Sawyer and his Aunt Polly and his brother Sid, and lots of others.

(5) It was after eight o'clock when I woke up the next day and the sun was high in the sky.

(6) Carefully, I looked through the trees, and I saw a boat full of people.

(7) I found a good place under the trees to sleep and to put my things.

(8) I watched them, but they didn't see me, and in the end they went away.

(9) I knew that nobody was going to come and look for me again.

(10) Then I caught a fish and cooked it over a fire.

Text A  My Deep，Dark Secret

Vocabulary related to Text A

Additional Tasks

1. **Word Formation.**

   1）**Study how the word "monitress" is formed. Find out the meaning of the suffix "-ess" with the help of a dictionary.**

   monitress：monitor（male）→ monitress（female）

   Fill out the table below，changing the given nouns（male）into nouns（female）by adding the suffix "-ess".

   Example：actor（male）（*n.*）→ actress（female）（*n.*）

nouns（male）	nouns（female）	nouns（male）	nouns（female）
leopard		host	
steward		waiter	
tiger		emperor	
prince		author	
lion		doctor	

   2）**Study how the word "decode" is formed. Find out the meaning of the prefix "de-" with the help of a dictionary.**

   decode：de＋code（*n.*）→ decode（*v.*）

   Fill out the table below，changing the given nouns into verbs by adding the prefix "de-".

54

Example： <u>de</u>＋<u>cipher</u> （*n.*）→ decipher （*v.*）

nouns	verbs	nouns	verbs
fame		bug	
forest		ice	
form		value	
frost		bone	
control		colour	

3）Translate the following phrases into English，using words with the suffix "-ess" or prefix "de-".

（1）女主人的邀请

（2）去除鸡骨

（3）女乘务员迷人的微笑

（4）乱伐森林的后果

（5）女服务员的服务态度

（6）去除电脑中的病毒

（7）公主的婚礼

（8）为冰箱除霜

（9）母狮的幼崽

（10）解除物价管制

2. Complete the sentences with the following expressions. Use the proper forms.

turn out	balk at	take every opportunity	compensate for
on special occasions	once in a while	on a ... basis	buy into

（1）We meet for lunch _____ since we are so busy with work.

（2）I don't _____ all that New Age stuff.

（3）I have a suit but I only wear it _____.

（4）I _____ the prospect of spending four hours on a train with such a nasty person.

（5）Victims of the crash will be _____ their injuries.

（6）Her granddaughter has _____ to be very musical.

（7）Most of our staff work for us _____ voluntary _____.

（8）Ann _____ of visiting her parents when she lived in the same city with them.

3. Complete the following sentences with the correct word.

1） to abandon　　to desert　　to leave

（1）The cruel man _____ his wife and child.

（2）My brother _____ the advertising profession but continued to mix with agency people.

（3）The hunter _____ his injured friends.

2） to amuse　　to entertain　　to interest

(1) The showing of slides _____ the dozing student, and he sat up and took notice.

(2) She _____ herself by reading detective stories.

(3) The magician _____ the children with a variety of tricks.

3) to answer   to reply   to respond

(1) The boss _____, "in that case you should have caught the earlier bus."

(2) I received her letter a month ago but have not _____ a word.

(3) Be always ready to _____ provocations (挑衅) of invaders with head-on blows.

4) to ask   to inquire   to question

(1) They _____ the reason of his long absence.

(2) It cannot be _____ that the new method is superior to the old one.

(3) She _____ of me how to proceed with the work.

5) to attempt   to struggle   to try

(1) We should give moral support to those who _____ to build a new society.

(2) You can _____ out a new recipe for pudding.

(3) The British troops were driven back when they _____ to break through the enemy's line.

4. **Complete the sentences with the following verbal phrases in their proper forms.**

tell against	tell apart	tell from	tell off	tell on
see about	see to	see off	see over	see through

(1) His mother _____ him _____ for not doing his homework.

(2) It's a reputation that might _____ him if he ever decides to change jobs.

(3) He'd been three months in the job and the strain was beginning to _____ him.

(4) I've always had a problem with _____ my left _____ my right.

(5) It's impossible to _____ a forged £10 note _____ from a real one.

(6) Some people are coming to _____ our house tomorrow.

(7) Please _____ it that no one enters without identification.

(8) You should _____ getting your hair cut.

(9) She was so convincing that I didn't _____ her lies until it was too late.

(10) My parents came to the airport to _____ me _____.

5. **Examine the meanings and uses of "apply" and "subtle" in the sentences below. List other possible ways of using these words, and then make sentences after the models.**

When it came time for graduate school, I *applied* all over the county. (Para. 4)

I had internalized the not-so-*subtle* message that once you reach your magical 18 birthday, you should be completely self-reliant. (Para. 7)

(1) We've **applied** to a charitable organization for a grant for the project.

(2) Those were old regulations — they don't **apply** any more.

(3) **Apply** the suntan cream liberally to exposed areas every three hours and after swimming.

(4) He wants a job in which he can **apply** his foreign languages.

(5) You can solve any problem if you **apply** yourself.

(6) The play's message is perhaps too **subtle** to be understood by young children.

(7) There is a **subtle** difference between these two plans.

(8) Hughes was a nice man, but not a **subtle** one.

(9) His whole attitude had undergone a **subtle** change.

(10) There are some new **subtle** pastels (彩笔) on the table.

Other possible uses of "apply" and "subtle".

apply：

subtle：

6. Translate the following into English, using the words and expressions given in the brackets.
(1) 他阅历不深,但行事明理。(maturity)
(2) 年轻人往往以轻蔑的目光看待这种努力。(disdain)
(3) 他们忽视了其中牵涉的巨大危险。(overlook)
(4) 这是我们对以后几星期的临时安排。(temporary)
(5) 大卫向我保证他是个出色的登山者。(assure)
(6) 各工会必须优先考虑保护会员们的利益。(give priority to)
(7) 他已经发现了一种可以通过绘画表达自己观念和经历的方法。(perception)
(8) 他对青少年的心态有独特的理解。(unique)
(9) 他们继续与逆境搏斗。(adversity)
(10) 产业界应该用最为切实可行的好办法减少污染。(abate)

7. Cloze.

There are more women with M. B. A. 's and high-tech degrees. In 1997, women ___1___ 39% of all graduate business and management degrees, JoMei Chang, 47, the CEO of Vitria Technology — a $5 billion company ___2___ in applications integration software — has watched the ranks of women in high-tech grow as well. In 1984, when she arrived at a small silicon Valley start-up with a Ph. D. , she found herself the only female engineer on a 20 - person team. ___3___ last year, when she was asked back to speak, her hosts couldn't tell her how much those ranks had ___4___ .

Today, the greatest challenge to women entrepreneurs is the difficulty of managing both a company and a family. Heather Blease, 37, who founded Envision Net five years ago, can speak to those ___5___ drags. At a time when her company was ___6___ from three to 1,500 employees, she was changing diapers for three toddlers under 6. Leaving for one crucial fundraising trip to the West Coast, her second son demanded, "Mommy, do you love your company ___7___ than me?" She ___8___ that moment.

But no female entrepreneurs ___9___ that such warring demands are without a price. Kurtzig admits her work played ___10___ small part in her divorce. Still, she now urges young women M.B.A. students to "Go for it".

(1) A. deserved   B. demanded   C. earned   D. enjoyed

(2) A. generalizing   B. particularizing   C. specializing   D. summarizing

(3) A. In   B. At   C. During   D. By

(4) A. swelled   B. intensified   C. magnified   D. stretched

(5) A. contending   B. colliding   C. conflicting   D. opposing

(6) A. succeeding   B. progressing   C. broadening   D. exploding

(7) A. more   B. rather   C. other   D. else than

(8) A. got over   B. got around   C. got at   D. got across

(9) A. suspect   B. suppose   C. allege   D. pretend

(10) A. much   B. no   C. any   D. neither

Grammar   related to Text A   **Additional Tasks**

1. Read the following sentences carefully and then translate them into proper Chinese.

(1) My trip to America is *more than* sightseeing.

(2) This is *more than* I can tell.

(3) A whale is *no more* a fish *than* a horse is.

(4) The child was *more* frightened *than* hurt.

(5) She is *more* shy *than* cold.

(6) It is even *more* a poem *than* a picture.

(7) I'm *more than* happy to take you there in my car.

(8) He dismissed Bryan as *nothing more than* an amateur.

2. Translate the following sentences into English, using the patterns given in the brackets.

(1) 他们非常乐意帮忙。(more than)

(2) 与其说她愚蠢，还不如说她疯狂。(more ... than)

（3）你同我一样都不会讲汉语。（no more ... than）

（4）那同洗个淋浴一样。（nothing more than）

（5）他只不过要有人同他聊聊。（nothing more than）

（6）你们会有足够的钱去买你们所需要的任何设备。（more than）

（7）这是个十分慷慨的安排。（more than）

（8）心情舒畅将能充分补偿你可能遭受到的任何损失。（more than）

Writing Task related to Text A

Additional Tasks

The first and last sentences of the following story are missing. Work individually or in a group, and choose the best first and last sentence from those below the story. Decide what makes a good first sentence and a good last sentence.

_____ A few years ago I spent a week in the Dominican Republic. The week was over, and I was at the airport ready to leave when I discovered, to my dismay, that I had forgotten one of my suitcases at my hotel. Quickly, I jumped into a taxi and explained my situation to the taxi driver. We sped off in the direction of my hotel. Suddenly, the taxi driver slowed down so he could talk with the driver of a truck moving along the road next to us. The truck contained live chickens. Without stopping the taxi, the taxi driver stuck his hand out the window and took a live chicken, which he neatly stuck under the seat next to him. Meanwhile, I was getting more and more anxious about my suitcase and making my plane on time. Time wasn't bothering the taxi driver, though. Instead of heading straight for the hotel, he made a detour to drop the chicken off at his home! In the end, however, we managed to get the suitcase and then raced back to the airport. Fortunately, I made it to my plane on time. _____

Choices for the first sentence:

A. There are lots of things to do in the Dominican Republic if you have enough time.

B. Traveling can have its exciting, though frustrating moments.

C. I've always enjoyed traveling.

D. I often go to the Dominican Republic, and I always take a taxi from the airport to my hotel.

Choices for the last sentence:

A. That was the second time I'd been to the Dominican Republic; the first time was eight years ago.

B. Airline connections to the Dominican Republic are fairly good.

C. Travel is a difficult thing.

D. What started out as a frustrating moment ended up being a happy memory and a great story.

Unit 1

Text A  The Cab Ride

Vocabulary | related to Text A

Additional Tasks

1. Word Formation.

1) **Study how the word "neighborhood" is formed. Find out the meaning of the suffix "-hood" with the help of a dictionary.**

neighborhood: <u>neighbor</u>+<u>hood</u>

Add suffix "-hood" to the following words. Pay attention to the change of the meaning of the words. Add more words to the list.

Example: boy+hood → boyhood (the state or the period of being a boy)

brother		man	
child		false	
king		god	
likely		sister	
lively		woman	

2) **Study how the word "industrial" is formed. Find out the meaning of the suffix "-ial" with the help of a dictionary.**

industrial: <u>industry</u>+<u>ial</u> (changing "*y*" into "*i*")

Fill in the table below, changing the given nouns into adjectives by adding the suffix "-ial", and adjectives into nouns by deleting the suffix.

Example: race (*n.*) → rac*ial* (*a.*)

nouns	adjectives	nouns	adjectives
agent			remedy
ceremony			adverbial
face			colonial
influence			financial
manager			official
part			proverbial
preference			territorial

3) **Complete the sentences based on the Chinese given in the brackets.**

(1) He has grown into a big guy. But he can still remember his _____ (孩提时代) wishes.

(2) Though the brothers drifted apart as they grew up, their _____ (兄弟情谊) remained.

(3) In all _____ (可能性), it will snow.

(4) He earned his _____ (生计) by painting.

(5) In times of _____ (财政的) difficulty the university has a duty to decide where money can be saved.

(6) She was _____ (有影响力的) in persuading government to enact the new law.

(7) The referee was _____ (偏向于) to the home team.

(8) The hotel gives _____ (优惠的) treatment to people who stay in it regularly.

(9) Arabic is the _____ (官方正式的) language of Morocco.

(10) The candidates for that position are expected to have rich _____ (管理的) experience.

2. **Complete the sentences with the following expressions. Use the proper forms.**

be conditioned to	depend on	make a living	reach into
hold onto	shut off	revolve around	

(1) Even the older members of the party have _____ their youth idealism.

(2) Gas supplies were _____ for four hours while the leak was repaired.

(3) My life mainly _____ my job and my family.

(4) A house in this area will cost between 60,000 dollars and 80,000 dollars, _____ its size and condition.

(5) She _____ by painting.

(6) He _____ his inside coat pocket and produced a pen.

(7) He _____ flare up (发火) over trifles.

3. **Complete the sentences with the following verbal phrases in their proper forms. Some phrases can be used more than once.**

pick at	pick off	pick on	pick out	pick over
pick through	pick up	pick up after	pick ... up on	

(1) Keep the room tidy! Don't always expect me to _____ you.

(2) A team of investigators _____ the wreckage of the plane, trying to discover the cause of the crash.

(3) She sat nervously in the dentist's waiting-room, _____ the sleeve of her jumper.

(4) By the time I got to the sales, most of the clothes had already been _____.

(5) I _____ quite a lot of Spanish during my six-month stay in Madrid.

(6) Parents who smoke should discourage their children from _____ the habit.

(7) My Spanish teacher always _____ me _____ my pronunciation.

(8) A witness _____ the attacker from police photos.

(9) He was _____ at school because he was much smaller than the other kids.

(10) Several leading British scientists have been _____ by the American universities.

4. **Examine the meanings and uses of "hold" and "depend" in the sentences below. List other possible ways of using these words, and then make sentences after the models.**

She *held* onto me tightly. (Para. 18)

But I had seen too many impoverished people who *depended* on taxis as their only means of transportation. (Para. 5)

(1) He had difficulty in **holding** the teapot steady when he poured out the tea.

(2) We have **hold** the job open for him for one week now.

(3) **Hold** your tongue!

(4) The arrested students **were held** without trial from 84 days to six months.

(5) I **hold** the view that he is an honest man.

(6) We have enough food to **hold** us for one month.

(7) Success **depends** on your efforts and ability.

(8) The old man **depended** on her daughter to keep the house.

(9) A: Do you always go on your holiday together with your sister?

B: It **depends**. If I have my holiday at the same time as she, then we go together.

(10) Matters of the greatest moment were **depending**.

Other possible uses of "hold" and "depend".
hold：

depend：

5. **Put the following into English，using the words and expressions given in the brackets.**
   (1) 哥白尼推论说地球绕太阳运转。(reason, revolve round)
   (2) 夜班工人六点来到。(shift)
   (3) 船正向岸边驶去。(head)
   (4) 在激烈的竞争中,该公司正渐渐被挤出这个市场。(squeeze)
   (5) 这架飞机对其操纵系统反应灵敏。(respond)
   (6) 我预料在做这件工作中会遇到很多困难。(encounter)
   (7) 那些政客们对这项调查并不十分热心。(solicitous)
   (8) 我的手伸不进那管子,它太窄了。(reach into)
   (9) 她形成了以我为敌的习惯。(be conditioned to)

6. **Fill in the missing words.**

   The ___(1)___ includes birth, aging and death, and death is the inevitable ___(2)___ of life. Aging is the neglected stepchild of the human life cycle. Death comes within seconds ___(3)___ old age is a long ___(4)___ which includes illnesses, poverty and isolation. Advertisements and travel folders show relaxed, happy, well-dressed older people enjoying recreation, travel and their grandchildren. But it is ___(5)___ for the poor elderly to enjoy them. They have to struggle ___(6)___ survival when ___(7)___ old. For the most ___(8)___ the elderly struggle to exist in an inhospitable world. Now older people are ___(9)___ the increase in the world, and problems with elderly are arousing ___(10)___ among governments of many countries.

> **Grammar** related to Text A

Additional Tasks

1. **Fill in the blankets with the proper form of the verbs，paying attention to the structure：** *have (make) sb. do sth. , get sb. to do sth. , have sb. doing sth. , have (get) sth. done.*
   Model：

   She *had me pull up* in front of a furniture warehouse ... (Para. 12)
   (1) The boss often has them _____ (work) for 14 hours a day.
   (2) You'd better have your car _____ (run) slowly.
   (3) Don't have the baby _____ (cry).
   (4) I got him _____ (help) me when I moved the furniture.
   (5) She is made _____ (clean) the washing room.

(6) Don't forget to have Mr. Brown _____ (come) to our party.

(7) I want to have my computer system _____ (update).

(8) Don't have the dog _____ (bark) much, Lilin.

(9) The patient is going to have his temperature _____ (take).

(10) If you are too busy, I can get someone else _____ (type) it.

Writing Task | related to Text A

Rearrange the sentence order and translate them into Chinese.

1. She turned towards the door and saw me.

2. After I went in and sat down, she returned to her knitting.

3. The door of her room was open, and I saw a tiny woman sitting in an armchair beside the bed, knitting something that didn't look like anything.

4. She looked at me for a while and then nodded her head and patted the bed.

5. "May I come in?" I asked.

6. But she didn't look up for she obviously couldn't hear well.

7. She didn't answer my last question.

8. "What are you knitting?" I asked.

9. "Nothing", she turned up her wrinkled face and answered.

10. I thought she was a bit crazy, so five minutes later I thanked her and left.

11. She continued knitting clumsily and diligently.

12. "May I come in?" I raised my voice this time.

13. "Nothing? Why are you knitting then?" I asked.

14. A few days later, I received a note which said:
    Dear John,
    The woman you met here asked that we send you this gift, and she wanted to thank you for visiting her. She died three days ago. She was very happy.

Text A  Civilization and History

Vocabulary | related to Text A

Additional Tasks

1. **Word Formation.**

1) **Study how the word "industrious" is formed. Find out the meaning of the suffix "-ous" with the help of a dictionary.**

industrious: industry+ous

Fill out the table below, changing the given nouns into adjectives by adding the suffix "-ous".

Example: peril (*n.*) + ous → perilous (*a.*)

nouns	adjectives	nouns	adjectives
danger		prosperity	
vigor		glory	
luxury		curiosity	
ridicule		advantage	
marvel		adventure	

2) **Study how the word "predestined" is formed. Find out the meaning of the prefix "pre-" with the help of a dictionary.**

determiner: pre+determiner

Turn the following nouns into nouns that begin with the prefix "pre". Add more words to the list.

nouns	nouns	nouns	nouns
supposition		meditation	
fabrication		condition	
conception		school	
history		war	
industry		trial	

3）Complete the sentences based on the Chinese given in the brackets.

(1) A _____ （预审的）report recommended a higher sentence，she noted.

(2) He tries to deny information that challenges his _____ （先入之见）.

(3) The door of his study was open，and without _____ （预先考虑）he turned into it.

(4) Her mother provided her with _____ （奢侈的）clothes and food.

(5) It is _____ （奇怪的）how two such different problems can be solved so similarly.

(6) The audience were enthusiastic about this _____ （绝妙的）invention.

(7) The League remained in overt and _____ （强烈的）opposition to the war.

(8) Redistribution is a _____ （先决条件）for any transition to a stable society.

(9) They charge you a _____ （荒唐的）price.

(10) People can be persuaded to believe things which contradict their former _____ （预先假定的事）.

2. Complete the sentences with the following expressions. Use the proper forms.

rule over	be good at	after all	settle one's disputes	other than
kill off	point of view	scale ... down	oceans of time	on the whole

(1) The operations were _____ because the number of the enemy was diminishing.

(2) Tom is quite _____ mathematics，but when it comes to English，he often feels tired of it.

(3) It's a pity that some college students spend _____ playing video games.

(4) We want to hear the _____ of ordinary people on this project.

(5) There was no noise _____ a muted organ.

(6) George Ⅲ _____ Great Britain for 60 years.

(7) They did not expect heavy losses in the air；_____ , they had superb aircraft.

(8) _____ he is a very difficult character.

(9) This discovery _____ one of the last surviving romances about the place.

(10) Many countries try to _____ with other countries by diplomacy.

3. Complete the sentences with the following verbal phrases in their proper forms.

break away	break down	break in	break off	break out
break through	break up	break out of		

(1) Their marriage _____ after their two years' quarrel.

(2) He was said to be an innovative musician _____ from the classical tradition.

(3) They told the police that they had _____ through a gardener's gate.

(4) The clerks in this company are allowed to _____ for a cup of coffee every day.

(5) They tactfully _____ her reserve in the negotiation.

(6) Fierce fighting _____ between rival groups owing to their disagreement on the treaty.

(7) The peace talks _____ without any agreement being reached.

(8) They finally _____ the vicious cycle after they got some knowledge about the matter.

(9) The sun managed to _____ for a while that afternoon.

(10) Water is readily _____ into hydrogen and oxygen.

4. Examine the meanings and uses of "figure" and "grasp" in the sentences below. List other possible ways of using these words, and then make sentences after the models.

People think a great deal of them, so much so that on all the highest pillars in the great cities of the world you will find the *figure* of a conqueror or a general or a soldier. (Para. 1)

These figures are difficult to *grasp*; so let us scale them down. (Para. 3)

(1) Those **figures** indicate why the black people live in such deep poverty.

(2) They're asking a high **figure** for their house.

(3) His political activity made him a powerful **figure** in Russian culture.

(4) A **figure** loomed up out of the mist.

(5) She had an excellent **figure** and walked with an air.

(6) This controversy was expected to **figure** importantly in their discussion.

(7) He **grasped** the opportunity to ask for a higher salary.

(8) They failed to **grasp** the full significance of these events.

(9) The drowning man **grasped** at a branch.

(10) The country is in the **grasp** of a dictator.

Other possible uses of "figure" and "grasp".

figure:

grasp:

5. Translate the following into English, using the words given in the brackets.

(1) 其他任何人都会认为这些规定行不通。(reckon)

(2) 在过去的 25 年中他们未能维护法律和社会治安。(maintain)

(3) 这是我所见过的最为雍容华贵的花卉。(glorious)

(4) 在多次攀登尝试后,终于有人在 1985 年登上了这座山的顶峰。(conquer)

(5) 他在袭击和残害这些妇女时神经一时失常了。(mutilate)

(6) 他和她素不相识,被人强迫而只得驾车送她回家。(bully)

(7) 去年秋天推出的一系列新产品已经很畅销。(launch)

(8) 她是个软弱而没有骨气的人。(creature)

(9) 有过大量的辩论,而问题还是没有解决。(dispute)

(10) 文化与社会的演变如今已变得极为迅速。(evolution)

6. Cloze.

　　Travel writing involves an odd social contract: writer, for pay, agrees to view inspirational scenery and have a great time, saving readers the trouble of doing so. But Mark Hertsgaard's contract was odder than most. A Few years ago, the journalist, set off on a trip around the world in search of noxious vistas and pollutive sunsets — the environmental wreckage that other travelers take ___(1)___ to avoid. His clear-eyed report, ___(2)___ by careful scholarship, is one of the best environmental books in recent years. It may help save readers the trouble of living ___(3)___ ecological decline and fall, if enough of them ___(4)___ how and where to apply its bitter lessons.

　　When Hertsgaard travels to western Ethiopia and sees starving refugees, there's not much to say except that life is cruel. They were ___(5)___ from their home in Sudan by drought and war. It is in Bangkok, strangely enough, ___(6)___ the message of Hertsgaard's journeying begins to strike home. This sprawling river city is like most others — mad about cars, ___(7)___ by car traffic, its air made unbreathable by cars and its municipal life dying of cars. If this ___(8)___ all, the moral would be simple: avoid Bangkok. Yet cars there, and across Europe and especially in the U. S., are efficient carbon ___(9)___ . And carbon dioxide is the main ingredient in the greenhouse shield that is warming the globe and adding ___(10)___ energy to epochal storms and floods.

(1) A. effects   B. pains   C. strains   D. forces

(2) A. backed   B. advocated   C. boosted   D. assisted

(3) A. in   B. beyond   C. through   D. on

(4) A. account for   B. bring about   C. count on   D. figure out

(5) A. driven   B. exiled   C. banished   D. pulled

(6) A. where   B. what   C. whose   D. that

(7) A. disabled   B. weakened   C. paralyzed   D. aggravated

(8) A. were   B. was   C. had been   D. has been

(9) A. manufacturers B. generators   C. creators   D. removers

(10) A. furious   B. bleak   C. clamorous   D. roaring

Grammar   related to Text A

Rewrite the following sentences after the model, using the non-restrictive attributive clause.

Model:

1. They were invited to the state banquet. It was a great honour to them.
   They were invited to the state banquet, which was a great honour to them.

2. The West Lake is in Hangzhou. It is one of the world-famous scenic spots.
   The West Lake, which is one of the world-famous scenic spots, is in Hangzhou.

(1) London has a history of nearly two thousand years. It stands on the River Thames.

(2) She is going to marry Dick. She does not love him.

(3) They went on to Beijing. They stayed there for a week.

(4) We saw a church among the trees. Its tower was clear against the blue sky.

(5) He was a Frenchman. I could tell that from his accent.

(6) Foamglass resists heat, doesn't burn, and doesn't rot. This is true of all glass.

(7) He came at six. At that time I am usually in the garden.

(8) He did not believe me. I expected this.

(9) My dog often bites the visitors. Its temper is very uncertain.

(10) Another important source of income are the famous Andorran stamps. Most stamp collectors are familiar with this fact.

Writing Task   related to Text A

The following sentences form the opening paragraph of a story, but they are in the wrong order. Work with a group to put them in logical order.

_____ No one knows for sure when the ancestors of sea turtles first ambled off land and into the ocean.

_____ Hirayama believes the new find — about eight inches long — shows that the evolution of a salt-excreting system allowed these turtles to venture into the sea even before the complete development of rigid paddles.

_____ Like modern sea turtles *Santanachelys gaffneyi* had large glands near its eyes that secreted salt it absorbed from the sea, preventing dehydration.

_____ But this newly discovered, unusually complete, and exquisitely preserved sea turtle from a limestone deposit in Brazil answers key questions about that evolutionary journey, says Ren Hirayama of Japan's Teikyo Heisei University.

_____ But its limbs ended in primitive paddles with some movable digits, not the rigid paddles of today's sea turtles.

Text A  The Light Was On

Vocabulary | related to Text A

1. **Word Formation.**

   1）**Study how the word "multimedia" is formed. Find out the meaning of the prefix "multi-" with the help of a dictionary.**

   multimedia：multi＋media

   Turn the following adjectives into adjectives that begin with the prefix "multi-". Add more words to the list.

   Example： multi＋cultural → multicultural（*a.*）

adjectives	adjectives	nouns/adjectives	adjectives
national		dimensional	
racial		processing	
lingual		tasking	
lateral		storey	
coloured			

   2）**Study how the word "troublesome" is formed. Find out the meaning of the suffix "-some" with the help of a dictionary.**

   troublesome：trouble＋some

   Fill out the table below, changing the given nouns or adjectives or verbs into adjectives by adding the suffix "-some". Add more words to the list.

Example: whole＋some → wholesome (*a.*)

nouns/adjectives/verbs	adjectives	nouns/adjectives/verbs	adjectives
awe		venture	
bother		fear	
tire		lone	
loath		burden	
weary		irk	

3) **Complete the sentences based on the Chinese given in the brackets.**

(1) There is a new _____ (好冒险的) spirit among today's young people.

(2) New types of _____ (多重任务处理的) software are now available.

(3) What I hate about you most is the _____ (可恶的) way you use other people.

(4) The dog had a _____ (叫人害怕的) set of teeth.

(5) The handbook became more _____ (多民族化) in content as well as in ideology.

(6) The _____ (跨国的) mining giant has quietly bought up all the land in this area.

(7) Don't you know that boy is _____ (孤独)?

(8) We are in favour of the holding of bilateral or even _____ (多边的) talks.

(9) They are cut off from the rest of the world in a flat in a _____ (多层的) block.

(10) This suggestion ruled out any _____ (令人厌烦的) opposition from within.

2. **Complete the sentences with the following expressions. Use the proper forms.**

catch up on	allow for	go through
break up	sneak in	get through

(1) It's difficult to _____ to students who don't want to learn.

(2) The house was demolished to _____ road widening.

(3) They would be going straight to the office to _____ correspondence.

(4) You'd better _____ the names of the students who will attend the meeting.

(5) These games could be used to _____ the monotony.

(6) They watched the little girl _____ some of the movements she had learned.

(7) He will be qualified for the job if he _____ his two subjects this year.

(8) The burglar _____ when he was having a sound sleep last night.

(9) If you are self-employed，_____ tax and national insurance.

3. Complete the sentences with the following verbal phrases in their proper forms.

keep away	keep back	keep down	keep off	keep out of
keep to	keep under	keep up (with)	keep on	

(1) Pensions were increased to _____ the rise in prices.

(2) Please _____ the children _____ from the fire! It's dangerous.

(3) He _____ his bed when he had flu.

(4) For centuries men have been trying to _____ women _____.

(5) He _____ the question of whose fault it was.

(6) You _____ this. It's got nothing to do with you.

(7) You can't write an autobiography without _____ something _____.

(8) She can drink skimmed milk, but she has to _____ butter.

(9) Even friends have trouble _____ each other's whereabouts.

(10) Only half the workforce will be _____ after this order has been completed.

4. Examine the meanings and uses of "run" and "progress" in the sentences below. List other possible ways of using these words, and then make sentences after the models.

When I was in private practice as a pediatrician, life was always busy, and the days and nights often *ran* together. (Para. 1)

I put the water on to boil, and we began to chat. As the conversation *progressed*, we both began to share a little bit about ourselves, our worries and our frustrations. (Para. 4)

(1) The local college **runs** a course in self-defense.

(2) The government took desperate measures to keep the economy **running**.

(3) I turned the tap on and **ran** some cold water on the burn.

(4) Channel 4 is **running** a series on the unfairness of the legal system.

(5) Differences between the two sides **run** deep.

(6) The recent free elections mark the next step in the country's **progress** towards democracy.

(7) My Spanish never really **progressed** beyond the stage of being able to order drinks at the bar.

(8) As the war **progressed**, more and more countries became involved.

(9) Repair work is in **progress** on the south-bound lane of the motorway and will continue until June.

(10) We started off talking about the weather and gradually the conversation **progressed** to politics.

Other possible uses of "run" and "progress".

run:

progress：

5. **Translate the following into English，using the words given in the brackets.**
(1) 他需要聚精会神，不要干扰他的学习。(distract)
(2) 那个年轻女孩想当演员的愿望受到父母的阻挠，她很不愉快。(frustration)
(3) 请去向经理提意见，不要对我讲。(address)
(4) 和人交往时通情达理就会受人尊敬。(reasonable)
(5) 我将为你提供一则关于形势的新信息。(update)
(6) 张先生是那种性格直爽、好交际的人。(outgoing)
(7) 学生们把选修这门课看作是轻松的选择。(option)
(8) 我的弟弟并不出众，像他那样的年轻人比比皆是。(exceptional)
(9) 政府打算对整个税务制度进行改革。(contemplate)
(10) 发现它看来多半是出于偶然，而并非协同努力的结果。(fortuitous)

6. **Cloze.**

　　Today，I am going to talk about a common psychological problem caused by life in the modern world — burnout, which comes when the reality of life is less than our expectations.

　　School teachers and full-time housewives with children at home are among the highest risk groups ___(1)___ to suffer from burnout. The symptoms of the condition were first noticed among human service agency workers but the condition ___(2)___ everyone to a degree.

　　The burnout can be ___(3)___ into three stages. First is confusion. A worker may sometimes have chronic aches or colds. He may seem to lose his sense of humor and many things running through his mind makes him ___(4)___ in a discussion.

　　Cocoon phenomenon begins in the stage of moderate burnout which is characterized by more illness and absenteeism （走神）. In that state workers may have gray faces from three p.m. in the office until five, ___(5)___ a lot of clock-watching.

　　The third stage is ___(6)___ despair. There is depression and increase in drinking and risk-taking. The person ___(7)___ to pull into a shell, means he ___(8)___ work and social contact as much as possible.

　　___(9)___ burnout is mainly risk-related, it can occur in any of the multiple roles most people perform. People can learn some strategies to improve their skills ___(10)___ doing something about it.

(1) A. likable　　　　B. likely　　　　C. unlikely　　　D. likewise
(2) A. affects　　　　B. effects　　　　C. infects　　　　D. defects
(3) A. dispersed　　　B. separated　　　C. characterized　D. formed
(4) A. dizzy　　　　　B. inattentive　　C. dreamy　　　　D. indifferent
(5) A. accompanying　B. suffering　　　C. including　　　D. considering
(6) A. suggested　　　B. termed　　　　C. described　　　D. indicated
(7) A. proceeds　　　B. tends　　　　　C. speeds　　　　D. hastens

(8) A. cut down   B. cut off   C. cut through   D. cut up

(9) A. However   B. Although   C. Whatever   D. Even though

(10) A. at   B. in   C. on   D. with

Grammar | related to Text A

Additional Tasks

1. Rewrite the following sentences after the model, using the emphatic structure.

Model:

And it was that light that shone brightest on the night when Brian knocked at my office door. (Para. 11)

(1) My car was stolen. (强调主语)

(2) My family are going to Thailand on holiday. (强调宾语)

(3) The storekeeper sat down in that very place. (强调地点状语)

(4) We realize how important our eyes are only when we cannot see perfectly. (强调时间状语)

(5) They argued vociferously. (强调方式状语)

(6) We decided to return because she was ill. (强调原因状语)

(7) What made you so happy? (强调特殊疑问句)

(8) What kind of work do you want? (强调特殊疑问句)

(9) She eventually became a doctor. (强调表语)

(10) The price frightened me. (强调主语)

2. Observe how the verb "find" is used in the following sentences. Group them into types. Then make sentences by using the different structures.

(1) I usually found myself in the office late at night, just catching up on paperwork. (Para. 1)

(2) I found this time alone very peaceful. (Para. 1)

(3) He found two of the three windows smashed.

(4) He found Christine knitting there.

(5) We went to her house but we found her out.

(6) The invaders found the place a prosperous village and left it a scene of desolation.

(7) Did I tell you we have found a new long poem of Blake's?

(8) I found this to be true in all the cities I visited.

(9) I think I can find you something to do.

(10) Looking at his watch he found it was barely half past nine.

Additional Tasks

1. **Here is a paragraph which contains one sentence that is unrelated to the main idea, thus spoiling the unity of the paragraph. Would you please point out that sentence?**

   Pearls are gathered by men known as pearl divers. Actually, these men do not dive. They are lowered by a rope to the bottom of the sea. Many tourists in Japan enjoy shopping for cultured pearls. Pearl gatherers work in pairs, with one remaining at the surface to help the other return from his dive. An experienced pearl diver can stay down about a minute and a half and can often make as many as thirty dives in one day.

2. **Write a first-person narrative describing the happiest or saddest or most memorable or most important day in your life, for example, your first day at school, the day when you were given an interview, the day when you got your first pay, the day when someone (a teacher or a friend) walked into your life, or the day when something changed the course of your life.**

The Boy and the Bank Officer

Vocabulary related to Text A

Additional Tasks

1. Word Formation.

1) Study how the word "supercomputer" is formed. Find out the meaning of the prefix "super-" with the help of a dictionary.

supercomputer: super＋computer

Turn the following nouns into nouns that begin with the prefix "super-". Add more words to the list.

Example: super＋star → superstar (*n*.)

nouns	nouns	nouns	nouns
ego		model	
market		state	
power		highway	
structure		conductivity	
tanker		man	

2) Study how the word "womanish" is formed. Find out the meaning of the suffix "-ish" with the help of a dictionary.

womanish: woman＋ish

Fill out the table below, changing the given nouns or adjectives into adjectives by adding the suffix "-ish", and the adjectives into nouns or adjectives by deleting the suffix.

Example: red＋ish → reddish (*a.*)

nouns/adjectives	adjectives	nouns/adjectives	adjectives
dark			monkish
girl			kittenish
small			youngish
book			yellowish
man			brownish

3）Complete the sentences based on the Chinese given in the brackets.

(1) To succeed in that task you need to be a _____（超人）.

(2) We will give the boat a _____（暗色的）blue hull.

(3) A _____（年纪很轻的）man with long, blond hair was standing outside the hall.

(4) She was _____（雄赳赳的）, a sergeant-major in skirts.

(5) In the heavy seas her _____（上层结构）was almost awash.

(6) Who are the _____（超级大国）that currently dominate the world?

(7) He challenged the idea of woman's lack of _____（超我）, her independence upon the approval of others.

(8) She suddenly felt a surge of _____（少女似的）nervousness.

(9) Each leaf had several lighter _____（较浅的黄色的）patches on it.

(10) Do you really like those very thin _____（超级模特）?

2. Complete the sentences with the following expressions. Use the proper forms.

in the first place	on duty	as to	wear an expression
be aware of	hand over	shake … down	

(1) Police _____ the club _____, looking for narcotics.

(2) There were only two prison wardens _____ when the riot started.

(3) Most people are _____ the risks of investing in stocks.

(4) Britain was under no obligation to _____ that suspect _____ to America.

(5) Their faces _____ that said they were no longer afraid.

(6) There are many difficulties for me. _____ information will be difficult for me to obtain.

(7) John has been given no directions _____ what to write.

(8) In 1977 the problem was _____ to a computer.

(9) You can _____ at my place for tonight.

3. Complete the following sentences with the correct word.

1) desirable   desirous

    (1) It is really unbelievable that you're _____ of meeting the mayor.
    (2) That street is a _____ location for a large department store.
    (3) For this position it is _____ to know something about medicine.
    (4) Only after he began to work in the factory did he become _____ to study.

2) direct   immediate

    (1) Only _____ descendants can be immigrated into the country.
    (2) Can you tell me if there are any _____ flights to Athens?
    (3) The _____ cause of death is unknown.
    (4) Louis seems in no _____ danger, but that is all the doctor will tell us.

3) in the distance   at a distance

    (1) _____ there was heard again the lowing of the cattle.
    (2) There was a church _____ from the village.
    (3) You can see the ancient temple _____ of ten kilometres.

4) ensure   assure   insure

    (1) The cargoes were _____ against loss at sea.
    (2) Careful planning _____ her from harm.
    (3) These pills will _____ you a good night's sleep.
    (4) I can _____ you of my full support for your plan.

4. Complete the sentences with the following verbal phrases in their proper forms.

hold against	hold back	hold down	hold off	hold on to/onto
hold out	hold up	hold forth	hold out for	hold out on

(1) Luckily, the rain _____ and we had the party outside as planned.
(2) The longer the rebels _____ , the more publicity they'll receive for their cause.
(3) She wanted to disagree with what they were saying but something _____ her _____ .
(4) I'll be really angry if I find out you've been _____ me.
(5) He certainly made a mistake, but I don't _____ it _____ him.
(6) The roof was _____ by two steel posts.
(7) Car manufacturers are _____ their prices in an attempt to boost sales.
(8) The strike continues as post office workers continue to _____ better conditions.
(9) The path's rather steep here so you'll need to _____ the rail.
(10) She _____ on a variety of subjects all through lunch.

5. Translate the following words or phrases taken from the text into proper Chinese.
    (1) branch office   (2) the bank's policy

(3) the bank rules　　　　　　　(4) to represent the customer's interests

(5) a bank officer　　　　　　　(6) a bank teller

(7) deposit(s)　　　　　　　　　(8) withdrawal(s)

(9) to open an account　　　　　(10) savings account

(11) a checking account　　　　(12) a balance of $100

(13) to deposit one's money　　(14) to withdraw money from the bank

(15) to put money in the bank　(16) an open savings account book

6. **Examine the meanings and uses of "wear" and "account" in the sentences below. List other possible ways of using these words, and then make sentences after the models.**

He was holding an open savings-account book and *wearing* an expression of open dismay. (Para. 6)

"It's my money. I put it in. It's my *account*." (Para. 4)

(1) What are you **wearing** to Caroline's wedding?

(2) Some musicians don't like to **wear** rings when they're playing.

(3) The minister **wore** a confident smile throughout the interview.

(4) When she's working she **wears** her hair in a ponytail.

(5) The wheel bearings have **worn** over the years, which is what's causing the noise.

(6) I need to draw some money out of my **account**.

(7) Could you please pay/settle your **account** in full?

(8) He kept a detailed **account** of the suspect's movements.

(9) He doesn't drink alcohol on **account** of his health.

(10) She was **accounted** a genius by all who knew her work.

Other possible uses of "wear" and "account".

wear:

account:

7. **Translate the following into English, using the words given in the brackets.**
   (1) 车辆的噪音对城市居民是永无止境的骚扰。(irritation)
   (2) 他对摄影有强烈的爱好。(passion)
   (3) 我父母认为现在的年轻人不尊重权威。(authority)
   (4) 这孩子害怕那条外表凶恶的狗。(scare)
   (5) 我很佩服她能对错误的批评意见不予理会。(shrug)
   (6) 使我惊讶的是,他又犯了同样的错误。(dismay)
   (7) 假如你不讨厌无业游民,那你本身就有点是无业游民了。(loafer)

(8) 他每月在银行存一笔钱。(deposit)

(9) 她总是把事情弄糟;她是个不折不扣的大笨蛋。(idiot)

(10) 部队已经撤出危险地带。(withdraw)

8. Cloze.

A student may use a library in three ways. First, he may borrow books from it. Secondly, he may _____(1)_____ reference materials from its sections. Thirdly, he may use the library for general study purposes. In this lecture we shall examine aspects of the activities with a(n) _____(2)_____ to helping the students to use his library more easily and more _____(3)_____.

First, then, let's have a look at how books are borrowed. We _____(4)_____ that the student has already been given the author and the title of the book he wants to borrow, his first job is to go over the name _____(5)_____. This consists of a list of books entered on cards. These cards are placed _____(6)_____ alphabetical order under the name of the author, or editor by which the book is best known. The call number is the piece of information that enables the student to _____(7)_____ the book. It normally has two parts: the first part, or the class number, in the center, on the top line, tells you in what subject area the book _____(8)_____; the second part, or the author number, on the next line, gives the number _____(9)_____ to that specific author and that particular book. That is to say, while the class number tells the student which general area in the library to go to find the book, the author number will _____(10)_____ him to the exact shelf.

(1) A. confine   B. consult   C. confer   D. connect

(2) A. idea   B. opinion   C. attitude   D. view

(3) A. efficiently   B. positively   C. correctly   D. thoroughly

(4) A. surmise   B. predict   C. consider   D. assume

(5) A. catalogue   B. item   C. order   D. sheet

(6) A. on   B. in   C. of   D. with

(7) A. (seek) find   B. trace   C. locate   D. follow

(8) A. is included   B. includes   C. refers   D. is referred

(9) A. equal   B. relevant   C. identical   D. consistent

(10) A. direct   B. instruct   C. send   D. tell

Grammar related to Text A

Additional Tasks

1. Rewrite the following sentences after the model, using the prepositional phrase "*because of*" to show the reason.

Model:

The boy continued to hold my attention because of what happened next. (Para. 5)

(1) I said nothing about it because his wife was there.

(2) All flights have been cancelled because the fall of snow is so heavy.

(3) He lost his job because he was so careless.

(4) The rain was so heavy that the banks were broken.

(5) He was absent from class since he had a high fever.

(6) He retired last month because he was seriously ill.

(7) Because terrorists attacked this city frequently, many people were forced to leave this city.

(8) I couldn't see Helen's expression because her head was turned.

2. **Rewrite the following sentences after the model, using the structure "happen to".**

   Model:

   "The only difference is that a bank's goods happen to be money, which is yours in the first place. If banks were required to sell wallets and money belts, they might act less like churches." (Para. 1)

   (1) I met Mary at Tokyo airport when I was on business in Japan.

   (2) I bought this dictionary at a second-hand bookstore.

   (3) I learned some words of Spanish when I traveled in Spain.

   (4) Helen and I have the same date of birthday.

   (5) I once studied at the same university as Mr. Smith did.

   (6) There was a policeman on the corner, so I asked him the way.

   (7) If you see Jane, ask her to phone me.

   (8) The famous professor was out when his students paid a visit to him.

Writing Task | related to Text A >

Additional Tasks

1. **The following sentences form a paragraph, but they are in the wrong order. Work in a group, and put them in the right order.**

   (1) _____ The significance and meaning of the construction of the pyramids are uniquely sacred and religious.

   _____ The most important pyramids were not constructed by hordes of humiliated slaves (as an old legend relates), but by the mass of Egyptian farmers, who were motivated to participate in something sacred.

_____ The dead king had to continue to exist in the afterlife because he became divine (in part) and he had to assure the welfare and survival of his people.

_____ It took 100,000 men twenty years to build the Cheops Pyramid, and the exceptional system of provisioning must be admired.

_____ A pyramid is a huge but simple structure to commemorate a dead king.

_____ At this time the water came up to the desert and allowed the transportation of the blocks of stone almost to the place of work.

_____ There must be a highly organized system for all these workers to receive the necessary water, food, materials, and tools so that Cheops could be finished in time.

_____ Actual construction took place only when the Nile flooded and when field work was stopped.

2. Choose three to five pictures in series and then tell a story to your class by your imagination.

Text A  An Unforgettable Christmas

Vocabulary related to Text A

1. **Word Formation.**

   1) **Study how the word "overdue" is formed. Find out the meaning of the prefix "over-" with the help of a dictionary and translate the following words into Chinese.**

   overlook

   overwhelm

   overflow

   overtake

   overhead

   overpopulation

   overtime

   overturn

   2) **Fill out the table below, changing the given verbs into nouns by adding the suffix "-al", and the nouns into verbs by deleting the suffix.**

   Example: arrive (*v*.) +al → arrival (*n*.)

verbs	nouns	verbs	nouns
refuse			removal
propose			withdrawal
survive			signal
arrive			approval

3) Complete the sentences based on the Chinese given in the brackets.

(1) No difficulty can _____ (压倒) us.

(2) We can _____ (俯视) the whole of the harbor on the hillside.

(3) The flood _____ (淹没) the valley.

(4) They regard _____ (人口过剩) as a danger to society.

(5) These new orders for our manufactures will mean working _____ (加班).

(6) The approximate time of their _____ (到达) will be five o'clock.

(7) Your _____ (建议) is being actively considered.

(8) Attention should be paid to the protection of the environment for the _____ (生存) of precious and rare wild animals.

(9) He ordered us to cover the other comrades' _____ (撤退).

(10) We received a delicately worded _____ (谢绝) of our invitation.

2. Complete the sentences with the following words and expressions. Use the proper forms.

retrieve	fall apart	stand out	put out	on impulse
marvel at	handle	flight	a sheaf of	be inlaid with

(1) They used to be good friends, but _____ a few months ago.

(2) How do I _____ this without ruining our relationship?

(3) Henry had made his decision to fire me _____.

(4) One way to _____ a fire is to remove the supply of oxygen.

(5) Even the cleverest people _____ a child's ability to learn his native language in such a short time.

(6) He pulled open a drawer and took out _____ paper.

(7) This wall painting _____ gold and jade is very splendid.

(8) I ran back to _____ the bag I had left in the train.

(9) Her bright red hair made her _____ from the others.

(10) There was no lift and we had to climb six _____ of stairs.

3. Complete the sentences with the following verbal phrases in their proper forms.

put out	put aside	put down	put forward	put off
put on	put up	put up with	put through	

(1) You ought to have _____ some amount of money for a rainy day.

(2) The call has been _____, I can hear the telephone ring out at the other end, but no one answered.

(3) The flight was _____ because of ground fog.

(4) Noise is coming to the point where we can't _____ it.

(5) She _____ her hand to screen her eyes from the sun.

(6) But, when her version of the drama is _____ stage and receives applause, she would feel that everything she has done is well worth it.

(7) The point was _____ that we should check the inflation.

(8) I shall light a candle of understanding in the heart which shall not be _____.

(9) They _____ several tents by the lake.

(10) _____ the lunch _____ to my account.

4. **Examine the meanings and uses of "*handle*" and "*due*" in the sentences below. List other possible ways of using these words, and then make sentences after the models.**

I sat down in the streetcar, and there against the seat was a beautiful silk umbrella with a silver *handle* inlaid with gold and necks of bright enamel. I had never seen anything so lovely. (Para. 3)

My last job ended the day before Christmas, my thirty-dollar rent was soon *due*, and I had fifteen dollars to my name, which Peggy and I would need for food. (Para. 10)

(1) Linda was always giving me sincere advice, not on how to run the company, but on how to **handle** Henry.

(2) ATM (Automatic Teller Machine) is also applied to **handle** savings and credit cards.

(3) A hammer has a metal head and a wooden or metal **handle**.

(4) I gave a little pull at the door **handle** and it came off at once.

(5) This port **handles** 2 million tons of cargo each year.

(6) The concert was called off **due** to the storm.

(7) The bill is **due** on the first of next month.

(8) He received a large reward, which was no more than his **due**, i. e. at least what he deserved.

(9) China strictly protects the **due** rights of criminals.

(10) He is going bankrupt if he cannot pay off the loan that becomes **due** soon.

Other possible uses of "handle" and "due".

handle:

due:

5. **Translate the following into English, using the words and expressions given in the brackets.**

(1) 我已经长大了，可以处理我自己的事情。(handle)

(2) 如果没有电力供应,全世界的运输系统将陷于瘫痪。(fall apart)

(3) 一失足成千古恨。(on impulse)

(4) 和其他那些人比起来,她的才能很突出。(stand out)

(5) 我们对他那绝妙的钢琴演奏感到惊奇。(marvel at)

(6) 汽车损坏得很严重，要用很多钱才能修好。(be such that)

(7) 刚才准是下雨了。人行道都湿了。(must)

(8) 展厅里张挂着许多国画。(decorate)

(9) 如果你随手乱扔废物的话，就会破坏周围环境的自然美。(spoil)

(10) 因为大雾所有航班都已取消。(flights)

6. Cloze.

Some creatures exist because they are strong and can fight against their enemies. Their __(1)__ depends on their strength. They __(2)__ few young ones because few of these __(3)__ are killed. Lions, tigers, eagles are __(4)__, and they give birth to few young ones. A lion has only two __(5)__ three young ones each year.

Creatures which are __(6)__ and unable to defend themselves bring forth many young ones. Many of them are __(7)__ every year, but the race continues to exist __(8)__ so many young ones are produced. The race continues to exist __(9)__ of the numbers killed. Mice, rabbits, pigeons are creatures of this __(10)__.

One pair of pigeons give birth to thirty young ones in one year. __(11)__ fifteen of these are __(12)__ they will create fifteen multiplied (乘) by thirty, or four hundred and fifty pigeons in the second year. If they continue to multiply in this __(13)__ they will bring out 6,750 pigeons (225 multiplied by 30) in the third year. If they __(14)__ at the same rate, how many pigeons will be in the __(15)__ year? — Do the multiplication yourself. If pigeons went on reproducing at this rate, __(16)__ a few years the whole world __(17)__ be full of pigeons. All the crops would be eaten: all the fruit would be __(18)__. But they do not multiply so fast. Each year so many pigeons are killed __(19)__ the total number of pigeons in the world __(20)__ about the same. It neither increases nor decreases.

(1) A. existence   B. movement   C. living   D. behaviour
(2) A. make   B. give   C. bring   D. produce
(3) A. birds   B. tigers   C. animals   D. eagles
(4) A. healthy   B. cruel   C. strong   D. fierce
(5) A. either   B. or   C. but   D. and
(6) A. thin   B. sick   C. weak   D. stupid
(7) A. eaten   B. killed   C. injured   D. caught
(8) A. although   B. therefore   C. because   D. meanwhile
(9) A. in spite   B. instead   C. by way   D. consisting
(10) A. kind   B. like   C. place   D. range
(11) A. As   B. If   C. Since   D. Because
(12) A. babies   B. children   C. males   D. females
(13) A. way   B. course   C. route   D. direction
(14) A. go on   B. insist on   C. rise up   D. come down
(15) A. first   B. second   C. third   D. fourth

(16) A. by	B. within	C. after	D. without
(17) A. would	B. should	C. will	D. may
(18) A. consumed	B. wasted	C. harvested	D. destroyed
(19) A. which	B. that	C. as	D. so
(20) A. drops	B. grows	C. becomes	D. remains

1. Translate the following sentences with "times" into Chinese.

(1) Our classroom is *two times bigger* than theirs.

(2) Our classroom is *three times* as big as theirs.

(3) Its profits are rising *four times faster* than the average company.

(4) This new campus is *five times the size* of the old one.

(5) Mercury weighs about *fourteen times more* than water.

2. Improve the following sentences.

(1) She failed again in the English exam last week. She must be very lazy.

(2) They mustn't have gone out because the light is on.

(3) There should have someone on duty all the time.

(4) My wallet is nowhere to be found. I must drop it when I was on the bus.

(5) You can't have waken me up. I don't have to work today.

Put the following sentences in the right order to form a coherent passage.

(1) You go into the restaurant, pick up a tray, knife, fork, and spoon and queue at a counter where the food is on display.

(2) After paying, you take your tray to any table you like.

(3) And as there is no waiter you don't have to give a tip.

(4) You can have a good meal in ten minutes.

(5) If you are in a hurry and you want to have a quick meal there is no better than a self-service restaurant.

(6) You pick out what you want and put it on your tray, which you have to push along a special rack till you reach the cashier.

(7) The cashier will give you your bill.

(8) You can sit alone or with another customer.

Text A My Father's Music

Vocabulary related to Text A

Additional Tasks

1. Word Formation.

   1) **Study how the word "preface" is formed. Find out the meaning of the prefix "pre-" with the help of a dictionary.**

   preface: pre-+face

   Add the prefix "pre-" to the following words. Pay attention to the change of the meaning of the words. Add more words to the list.

   Example: pre+war → prewar

determine			preexist
view			precondition
mature			prepay
historical			precaution
school			prerequisite

   2) **Study how the word "engineer" is formed. Find out the meaning of the suffix "-eer" with the help of a dictionary.**

   engineer: engine+eer

   Fill out the table below, changing the given nouns or verbs into nouns by adding the suffix "-eer", and nouns into nouns, or verbs by deleting the suffix.

Example： cannon＋eer → cannoneer

nouns/verbs	nouns	nouns/verbs	nouns
musket		auction	
racket			profiteer
mountain			electioneer

3）**Complete the sentences based on the Chinese given in the brackets.**

　　(1) Take everything into consideration so that you will not make a ＿＿＿＿＿＿ (草率的,不成熟的) decision.

　　(2) Only a selected audience can watch the ＿＿＿＿＿＿ (预演) of the film.

　　(3) He took every ＿＿＿＿＿＿ (警惕) but still got a bad deal on that used car.

　　(4) This course is a ＿＿＿＿＿＿ (必需条件) to more advanced studies.

　　(5) The impact of the ＿＿＿＿＿＿ (学前的) education of a child cannot be ignored.

　　(6) Many retirees serve as ＿＿＿＿＿＿ (自愿者) in community service and day care centers.

　　(7) His grandfather was one of the ＿＿＿＿＿＿ (先驱) of flying.

　　(8) The ＿＿＿＿＿＿ (奸商,牟取暴利者) will lose the favor of their customers sooner or later.

　　(9) Mount Himalaya has been challenged by many ＿＿＿＿＿＿ (登山者).

　　(10) ＿＿＿＿＿＿ (从事竞选活动家) are those who work actively for a candidate or political party in an election campaign.

2. **Complete the sentences with the following expressions. Use the proper forms.**

embark on	carry away	hang on	spill out	dispose of
out of luck	out of character	under the spell of	rust away	drift off

　　(1) He ＿＿＿＿＿＿ into a daydream.

　　(2) May is a nice girl; her fit of temper was indeed ＿＿＿＿＿＿.

　　(3) I got a bit ＿＿＿＿＿＿ when I was dancing and got up on the table.

　　(4) We ＿＿＿＿＿＿ every word of the lecturer's.

　　(5) He has ＿＿＿＿＿＿ an adventure no one else has dared.

　　(6) His contribution was very great. It can never ＿＿＿＿＿＿.

　　(7) Nuclear waste is often ＿＿＿＿＿＿ under the sea.

　　(8) He listened quietly while she ＿＿＿＿＿＿ all her anger and despair.

　　(9) The forecast is not good, you may be ＿＿＿＿＿＿.

　　(10) Poor Snowwhite is ＿＿＿＿＿＿ of the bad witch.

3. **Fill in each blank with one of the two words or phrases from each pair and note the difference of meaning between them.**

　　1) special　　specific

(1) He has a _____ car because he cannot walk.

(2) Don't beat round the bush. I want a _____ answer.

2) conform   confirm

(1) On the first day when a pupil enters school, he is asked to _____ to the school rules.

(2) Please _____ your telephone message by writing to me.

3) ensure   insure

(1) It is advisable to _____ your life against accident.

(2) I fitted a new lock to _____ that the bicycle would not be stolen.

4) affect   infect

(1) The slight change of weather can _____ her delicate health.

(2) One of the boys in the class had a fever and he soon _____ other children.

5) sequence   consequence

(1) As a _____ of hospitalization, Shelly decided that she wanted to become a nurse.

(2) Please keep the cards in _____.

4. **Complete the sentences with the following verbal phrases in their proper forms.**

live by	live for	live in	live off	live on
live out	live through	live together	live up to	live with

(1) It was said that she had to _____ her last days in a nursing home.

(2) These people have decided not to _____ the society's rules.

(3) He and his family _____ 70 $ a week.

(4) She _____ her rich grandfather.

(5) The couple _____ each other.

(6) Such a bad reputation is hard to _____.

(7) The college is building a new accommodation block so that more students can _____.

(8) Did the trip _____ your expectations?

(9) For many years the population had _____ the threat of war.

(10) They _____ for two years before they got married.

5. **Examine the meanings and uses of "skip" and "coordinate" in the sentences below. List other possible ways of using these words, and then make sentences after the models.**

I wanted to *skip* the whole thing. (Para. 13)

I was able to string notes together and *coordinate* my hands to play simple songs. (Para. 10)

(1) He **skipped** aside to avoid another blow.

(2) I **skipped** (**over**) the uninteresting parts in the novel.

(3) The children **skipped** rope on the playground.

（4）John **skipped** the fourth grade.

（5）He **skipped through** the accounts before dinner.

（6）You have to **coordinate** the colors of your design.

（7）A good general manager can **coordinate** the functions of all sections of his company.

（8）She is a well-trained nurse who **coordinates** smoothly.

（9）Your muscles **coordinate** when you walk.

（10）Our efforts need to be further **coordinated** for higher efficiency.

Other possible uses of "skip" and "coordinate".

skip：

coordinate：

6. **Translate the following into English，using the words and expressions given in the brackets.**
   （1）我们在南安普敦(Southampton)上船，一星期后到达纽约下船。（embark）
   （2）当你打扫房间时，请把旧报纸处理掉。（dispose of）
   （3）她作为顾问每天乘火车上下班来往于剑桥和伦敦之间。（commute）
   （4）报纸读者可以选择自己感兴趣的新闻，略过自己认为枯燥或无关的消息。（skip）
   （5）他被胜利冲昏了头脑。（carry away）
   （6）几个星期来，我一直感到大祸即将临头。（impending）
   （7）她那件新裙子的设计，受到许多人称赞。（compliment）
   （8）她在手提包里摸索着寻找她的通行证。（fumble）
   （9）热带岛屿的美景把游客们给迷住了。（spell）
   （10）她的愤怒像火山爆发似的迸发出来。（spill out）

7. **Fill in the missing words.**

   Early upbringing in the home is naturally affected ___(1)___ by the cultural pattern of the community and by the parents' capabilities and their aims and ___(2)___ not only on upbringing and education but also on the innate ___(3)___ of the child. Wild differences of innate intelligence and temperament exist even in children of the ___(4)___ family. Parents can ascertain what is normal in physical, mental and social development, by ___(5)___ to some of the many books ___(6)___ on scientific knowledge in these areas, or by ___(7)___ notes with friends and relatives who have children. Intelligent parents, ___(8)___, realize that the particular setting of each family is unique, and ___(9)___ can be no rigid general rules. They use general information only ___(10)___ a guide in making decisions and solving problems.

Study the usage of adjoint adverbial in the models, then choose the answer that best completes each of the following sentences.

Model:

Fumbling for the right words, I thanked him for the legacy it took almost 30 years to discover. (Para. 18)

Seriously injured, Allen was rushed to the hospital.

1. _____ enough time and money, the researcher would have been able to discover more in this field.

   A. Giving   B. To give   C. Given   D. Being given

2. _____ at in this way, the present economic situation doesn't seem so gloomy.

   A. Looking   B. Looked   C. Having looked   D. To look

3. _____ at the picture, I couldn't help missing my middle school days.

   A. Looked   B. To look   C. Looking   D. Being looking

4. _____, she couldn't help crying.

   A. Having been deeply moved   B. Deeply moved

   C. To be deeply moved   D. Being deeply moved

5. _____, he can now only watch it on TV at home.

   A. Obtaining not a ticket for the match

   B. Not obtaining a ticket for the match

   C. Not having obtained a ticket for the match

   D. Not obtained a ticket for the match

6. _____ regular training in nursing, she could hardly cope with the work at first.

   A. Not received   B. Since receiving

   C. Having received   D. Not having received

7. Arriving at the bus stop, _____ waiting there.

   A. a lot of people were   B. he found a lot of people

   C. a lot of people   D. people were found

8. _____, it can't be forgotten.

   A. Once seen   B. Once is seen

   C. Once be seen   D. Being seen

9. _____, he left the room.

   A. Handed the paper   B. Handing in the paper

   C. Having handed the paper   D. Have handed the paper

10. _____, we found our way easily.

   A. Having been given a map   B. Given a map

   C. Being given a map   D. Be given a map

Additional Tasks

Rearrange the sentences in the right order to form a coherent passage and then translate it into Chinese.

1. As the ability to recognize and imitate rhythm develops, during ages four to five, children should be encouraged to accompany singing with melodic instruments (xylophone, autoharp, etc.).

2. For example, exposing children from birth to a variety of music in a broad range of tones and pitches will help them acquire the ability to distinguish differences in music, much as infants acquire the ability to distinguish their parents' native language (dialect) from a foreign language.

3. Learning music is much like learning a language, because there is a natural progression in development.

4. Although certain stages in child development are considered sensitive for developing specific musical and spatial abilities, no one blueprint will help your child become a master musician.

5. Then, during ages three to five, when children are developing better smooth muscle coordination and a sense of rhythm, they should be encouraged to sing along to music and engage in rhythmic activities, such as clapping, swinging, dancing, tapping, marching, and using nonmelodic instruments (rhythm sticks, cymbals, etc.).